Write Well 3

Practical Activities in Traditional and Functional Grammar Punctuation and Usage

Gordon Winch   Gregory Blaxell

Published by:
Horwitz Publications Pty Ltd.
55 Chandos Street St Leonards, NSW Australia 2065

Copyright © 1994 Gordon Winch and Gregory Blaxell

National Library of Australia Card No.
and ISBN 0 7253 1220 3
Series ISBN 0 7253 1224 6

COPYRIGHT
Apart from any fair dealing for the purposes of study, research, criticism or review, as permitted under the Copyright Act, no part of this book may be reproduced by any process without the prior permission of the publisher.

COPYING FOR EDUCATIONAL PURPOSES
Where copies of the part or whole of this book are made under Part VB of the Copyright Act, the law requires that records of such copying be kept and the copyright owner is entitled to claim payment.

Series Editor: Beverley Weynton
Illustrations: Jan Wade
Computer page composition: ID Studio, Sydney
Printed and bound in Australia by Alken Press, Smithfield

INTRODUCTION

The *Write Well: Practical Activities in Traditional and Functional Grammar, Punctuation and Usage* series covers the formal English skills which need to be mastered in the primary school. The workbooks are graded to cater for the level of every child and are keyed into *The Primary Grammar Handbook* which is the reference book to the series.

This book icon is located at the bottom of each page of this book. Within the book icon, the letters PGH refer to *The Primary Grammar Handbook*. There is also a number. This is the page reference to *The Primary Grammar Handbook*. So an icon with PGH 15 links that section of *Write Well 3* to page 15 of *The Primary Grammar Handbook*.

Each workbook contains units on traditional grammar, functional grammar including various genres, punctuation and correct English usage. The series responds to the challenge of providing materials which teach the essential skills of accurate spoken and written English.

The units in Book 3 are written in the context of the broad theme, Doing Things which includes specific themes on Holidays, That's Funny, Visits, Growing Things, Sport and Clothes. The units feature exercises which practise the skills and reinforce their use with a variety of interesting activites.

Answers to the exercises are provided in a central section of the book. This can be removed or left for immediate self-correction. A detailed Checklist is provided on the back page and a comprehensive Table of Contents allows for easy programming.

The *Write Well: Practical Activities in Traditional and Functional Grammar, Punctuation and Usage* series meets demand for material which places focus on mastery of the basic skills of English, skills which are part of the English syllabus of every state.

CONTENTS

FAMILY AND FRIENDS | UNIT 1 | Finding Nouns | 6

HOLIDAYS | UNIT 2 | Common and Proper Nouns | 8
| UNIT 3 | Collective and Abstract Nouns | 10
| UNIT 4 | Number with Nouns | 12
| UNIT 5 | Gender with Nouns | 14
| UNIT 6 | Agreement in Number | 16

THAT'S FUNNY | UNIT 7 | Recognising Personal Pronouns | 18
| UNIT 8 | Possessive Pronouns, Possessive Adjectives | 20
| UNIT 9 | Gender with Pronouns | 22
| UNIT 10 | Pronouns/Verbs Agree in Number | 24

VISITS | UNIT 11 | Descriptive Adjectives | 26
| UNIT 12 | Degree with Regular Adjectives | 28
| UNIT 13 | Degree with Irregular Adjectives | 30
| UNIT 14 | Adjectives for Nouns and Pronouns | 32
| UNIT 15 | Recognising Verbs | 34

GROWING THINGS | UNIT 16 | Tense in Simple Verbs | 36
| UNIT 17 | Present and Past Participles | 38
| UNIT 18 | Past Participles of Strong Verbs | 40
| UNIT 19 | Finding Adverbs | 42
| UNIT 20 | Types of Adverbs | 44

SPORT | UNIT 21 | Finding Prepositions | 46
| UNIT 22 | Using Prepositions | 48
| UNIT 23 | Prepositions and Pronouns | 50

CONTENTS

	UNIT 24	Recognising Conjunctions	52
	UNIT 25	Articles a, an, the	54
	UNIT 26	Articles and Interesting Adjectives	56
CLOTHES	UNIT 27	Interjections	58
	UNIT 28	Sentences and Non-sentences	60
DOING THINGS	UNIT 29	Recognising Phrases	62
	UNIT 30	Cohesion: Using Linking Words	64
	UNIT 31	Nominal Group: Building with Words	66
	UNIT 32	Genre: Recount	68
	UNIT 33	Genre: Instruction	70
	UNIT 34	Using Capital Letters	72
	UNIT 35	Using Full Stops	74
	UNIT 36	Using Question Marks	76
	UNIT 37	Using Exclamation Marks	78
	UNIT 38	Using Commas	80
	UNIT 39	More Using Commas	82
	UNIT 40	Quotation Marks	84
	UNIT 41	Double Negatives, Noun Plurals	86
	UNIT 42	Homonyms: Aren't, Aunt; and Others	88
	UNIT 43	Homonyms: Chews, Choose; and Others	90
	UNIT 44	Homonyms: Hole, Whole; and Others	92
	UNIT 45	Confused Words: A.M., P.M.; and Others	94
	UNIT 46	Confused Words: Loose, Lose; and Others	96
	UNIT 47	Confused Words: Ran, Run; and Others	98
	UNIT 48	Confused Words: Began, Begun; and Others	100
	UNIT 49	Confused Words: Broke, Broken; and Others	102

UNIT 1

FINDING NOUNS

> A *noun* is the name of a person, place or thing.

1 Underline the nouns in this poem, then write them in the spaces. The first one is done for you.

I NEED MY NOSE

I need my nose
To smell a rose;
My teeth to eat a pie.
I need my ear
To let me hear;
To see I need my eye.

I need my skin
To hold me in;
My feet so I can walk.
I need my lip
To let me sip;
I need my tongue to talk.

Gordon Winch

nose _____

_____

2 These are names of some family members. Write down any other family member nouns you can think of.

mother
father _____
brother _____

3 These are the given names of some family members. Write down the given names of the members of your family. Write them like this.

Mary—mother
John—father
Kylie—sister

_____

_____

4 Fill in the spaces with nouns.

My father's name is _____ . He has a red _____ .
My mother's name is _____ . Sometimes she drives the
_____ . At other times she rides her _____ . In school
holidays we go to the _____ and _____ . I can
swim very well now. We all wear _____ so we won't get
sunburnt. We swim between the _____ .

5 Add more nouns to these lists. Write them in the spaces.

chin	_____	James	_____	Emma	_____
hair	_____	Ali	_____	Carla	_____
nose	_____	Hamish	_____	Karen	_____
ear	_____	Mike	_____	June	_____
foot	_____	Li	_____	Meg	_____
_____	_____	_____	_____	_____	_____
_____	_____	_____	_____	_____	_____

6 Write down these nouns in the spaces.

Five things in your classroom. _____
_____

Five friends. _____
_____

Five sports or games you like to play. _____
_____

Five places you like to visit. _____
_____

COMMON AND PROPER NOUNS

Common nouns are the names of any common things. Common nouns start with small letters.
Proper nouns are the names of special people, places and things. They start with capital letters.

The word *beach* is a common noun.
The word *Bondi* is a proper noun.

1 Circle the common nouns in these sentences. Put rectangles around the proper nouns. The first two are done for you.

a. I like to go to the (beach) for holidays. My cousin, [Jane], comes with us. Last year we went to Mollymook.

b. We went to Mt Kosciusko last Christmas. Bill and Ali went with their parents. We climbed to the top.

c. My mother and father took us to Kakadu National Park. We pitched our tent and made damper. Joe Drake the ranger, waved to us from his Holden.

2 Write the nouns in the correct columns.

Common	Proper
beach	Jane

3 Fill in the spaces with proper nouns. Don't forget the capital letters.

We went to _____ Beach for our summer holidays. My friend, _____, came, too. We went on Monday and came back on _____. Dad drove our car, which is a _____. Our teacher, _____, asked me to tell the class about our holiday.

4 Write three common nouns in each box. The first one is done for you.

Camp	Beach	Zoo	Ferry
tent	_____	_____	_____
fire	_____	_____	_____
billy	_____	_____	_____

5 Write three proper nouns in each box.

Australian Cities	Australian States	Countries in the World	Places to Go For a Holiday
_____	_____	_____	_____
_____	_____	_____	_____
_____	_____	_____	_____

6 Finish these proper nouns.

Days	Months
Mon_____	Jan_____
Tues_____	Feb_____
_____day	Aug_____
_____day	Nov_____
_____day	Dec_____
_____day	
Sun_____	

Special Days

Aus_____ Day

Anz_____ Day

Christ_____ Day

UNIT 3 — HOLIDAYS
COLLECTIVE AND ABSTRACT NOUNS

A collective noun is a name given to a group of persons or things. In this sentence, *swarm* is a collective noun.

On my holidays, I was chased by a *swarm* of bees.

1 Finish these sentences by filling in the collective nouns.

a. I saw the l_____ of puppies.

b. The football t_____ won the match.

c. A s_____ of bees flew over our camp.

d. A h_____ of cattle was in the paddock.

e. We bought a b_____ of bananas.

2 Add the correct common nouns to finish these phrases.

a flock of _____

a school of _____

a choir of _____

3 Finish this paragraph with collective nouns.

On our holidays we watched the _____ of footballers win the match. We ate a whole _____ of bananas while the match was being played. Next day we went to see a new _____ of puppies. They had just been born and their eyes were closed. Then we went to see a movie. There was a big _____ of people outside and a bigger one inside.

An *abstract noun* is the name of something which is in your mind, although you can't see it.

Happiness is an abstract noun.

4 Write abstract nouns to match these pictures.

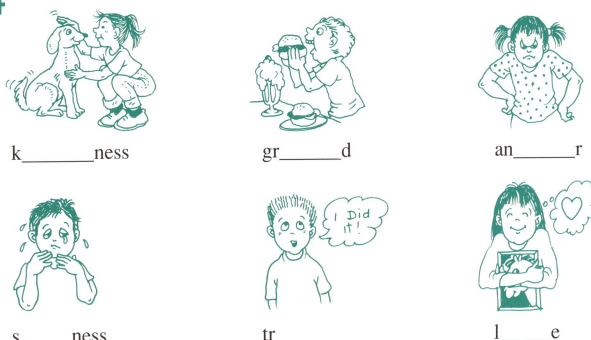

k_____ness   gr_____d   an_____r

s_____ness   tr_____   l_____e

5 Finish the abstract nouns in these sentences.

a. I was full of h_____ when I heard we were going away for a holiday.

b. When the boy hit my brother I was filled with an_____.

c. It is good to show k_____ to someone who needs help.

d. It is always best to tell the tr_____.

e. It was a time of s_____ when my puppy was sick.

6 Write a sentence for each of these abstract nouns.

kindness _____

truth _____

anger _____

UNIT 4

NUMBER WITH NOUNS

Nouns can be *singular* or *plural*. Singular means one; plural means more than one.

    one *holiday*   (SINGULAR)
    two *holidays*   (PLURAL)

1 Write the plurals of these nouns. The first one is done for you.

one tent   two __tents__

one car   two _____

one beach   two _____

one baby   two _____

one man   two _____

2 Write plural nouns in the spaces. Pick them from the singular nouns in the box.

We had _____ for lunch. For dinner we had baked _____ . There were seven _____ at our camping site. Mum had brought _____ and forks. She had a bread knife to cut the _____ of bread.

> tent
> sandwich
> potato
> knife
> loaf

3 Write the singular forms of these plural nouns.

ladies   _____   bees   _____

women   _____   sheep   _____

tomatoes   _____   mice   _____

spoonfuls   _____   stories   _____

chiefs   _____   ferries   _____

4 Do this wiggleword.

ACROSS
The plurals of:
2. watch
3. baby
4. loaf
6. herd
7. wolf

DOWN
The plurals of:
1. school
2. wife
3. beach
5. fox
6. heart

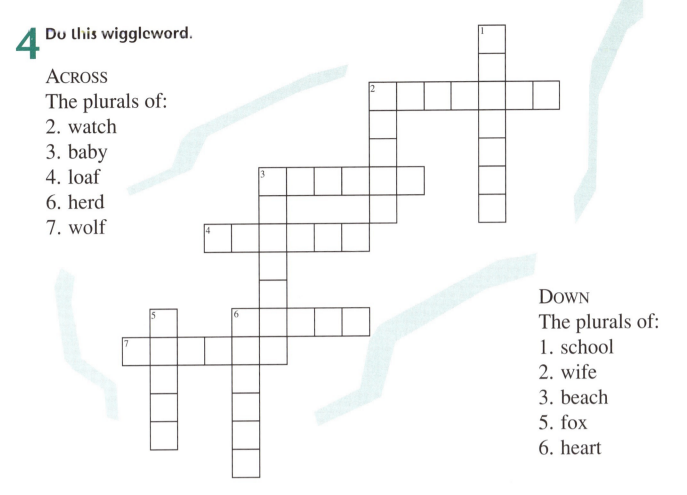

5 Make plurals with these wheels. Write the words in the spaces.

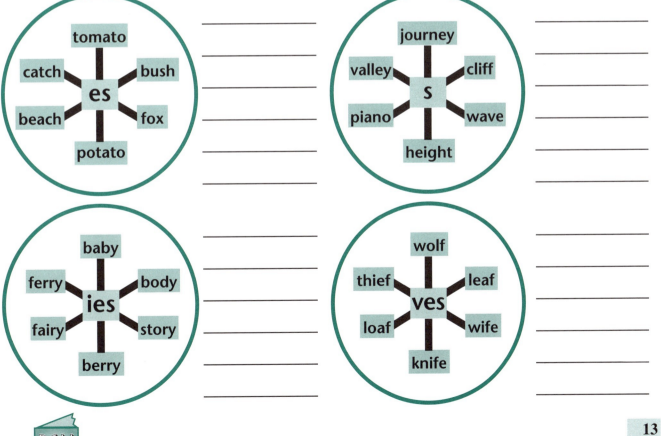

PGH 9

GENDER WITH NOUNS

UNIT 5 — HOLIDAYS

Nouns can be male or female. Male is masculine gender; female is feminine gender. If a noun is neither, it is *neuter gender*.

- **boy** — MASCULINE GENDER
- **girl** — FEMININE GENDER
- **holiday** — NEUTER GENDER

1 Read this paragraph. Underline the nouns. Write them in the spaces in three columns: masculine, feminine, neuter.

Angus and Jennifer went to the zoo. They ate hamburgers for lunch. They travelled on the ferry with Noni and Steve. Their mother and father went with them. Some waves splashed the rocks on the shore where some men and women were sitting.

MASCULINE	FEMININE	NEUTER
_____	_____	_____
_____	_____	_____
_____	_____	_____
_____	_____	_____
		_____
		_____
		_____

2 Write M F or N beside these nouns. (M for masculine, F for feminine, N for neuter.)

boy	____	cow	____	rock	____	niece	____
bicycle	____	bull	____	tent	____	actor	____
queen	____	rope	____	duck	____	grandfather	____
king	____	ram	____	girl	____	aunt	____
campfire	____	potato	____	bone	____	ewe	____

3 Write the feminine form of these masculine words. The first one is done for you.

boy	_girl_		uncle	_____
king	_____		prince	_____
tiger	_____		drake	_____
grandfather	_____		gentleman	_____
nephew	_____		brother	_____

4 Read this poem. Write M or F above each person. How many males went? How many females? Write the answers in the boxes.

FAMILY HOLIDAY

Father, mother,
Sister, brother,
Uncle Jim went, too.
Nephew, niece and Aunt Denise,
Cousins Jim and Sue.

Gordon Winch

M ☐

F ☐

Some nouns like *child* or *parent* include masculine and feminine. These nouns are said to be *common gender*.

5 Draw a circle around the nouns which are common gender.

a. The children were going to the country for their holidays.

b. The doctor was very kind to the patients.

c. The writer has won the prize.

d. The animals in the zoo seemed happy.

e. Our class visited the people who were in the hospital.

f. We visited the farm and saw the cattle, the sheep and the chickens.

UNIT 6

AGREEMENT IN NUMBER

Nouns must agree with verbs in number.

The *boy is*   The *boys are*

SINGULAR   PLURAL

You could not say, *the boy are* **or** *the boys is.*

The verb *is* **goes with singular nouns; the verb** *are* **goes with plural nouns.**

1 Cross out the wrong verbs in these sentences.
   a. The six tents (is, are) in a row.
   b. Our camp (was, were) in the forest.
   c. Five dogs (plays, play) on the beach.
   d. Swimming (is, are) the best fun.
   e. That man (was, were) eating the hamburger.

is   were
are   has
was   have

2 Fill in the spaces with words from the tent.
   a. Seven families _____ going on holidays.
   b. Mr Brown _____ going by himself.
   c. The six Smith children _____ at the camping site last year.
   d. Mario _____ four brothers and one sister.
   e. Five fish _____ caught by my dad and me. Mum _____ pleased.

Two or more singular nouns make a plural if they are joined by 'and'.

John and Ali *are* **friends.**

3 Cross out the wrong verbs in these sentences.

a. Tom and Jerry (is, are) funny.

b. Sydney and Melbourne (was, were) not here in the year 1700.

c. My mother and father (is, are) going to Japan for a holiday.

d. My sister and brother (play, plays) golf.

e. A ball, a bat and a wicket (is, are) needed for cricket.

4 Fill in the spaces with words from the ball.

a. Bill and Mary _____ very fast.

b. My dog and I _____ for a walk every evening.

c. Four calling birds, three French hens, two turtle doves and a partridge _____ all in one pear tree. Can you remember what other things _____ there, too?

d. Deer and cows both _____ horns.

run   was
runs   were
go   has
goes   have

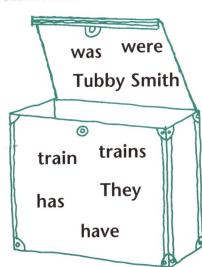

5 Finish these sentences. Pick from the box.

a. Jack and Jill _____ not very good hill climbers.

b. _____ are two good sportspersons.

c. _____ eats too much ice cream.

d. Top sportspersons _____ every day.

e. Five hundred runners _____ finished the race.

was   were
Tubby Smith
train   trains
         They
has
    have

UNIT 7 — THAT'S FUNNY

RECOGNISING PERSONAL PRONOUNS

A personal pronoun is used in place of a person or thing.

1 Circle the personal pronouns. The first one is done for you.

THE CLOWN

(I) like going to the circus. I like the lions, the elephants, the horses and the monkeys. They all do clever tricks. But most of all, I like the clown.

The last circus I saw, the clown's name was *Buttons*. He was very funny. He asked a girlfriend to help him. She was a good assistant. During their act, they played a joke on a kid from the audience. They asked this kid to look through a telescope. Then they poured water down the tube and the kid got wet. We all laughed.

Every circus has a clown. It must be a tough job being a clown. You have to be able to do so many things.

2 Write the personal pronouns.

_____

3 Fill in the spaces in these sentences. Choose from these personal pronouns: **I, he, she, it, we, you, they.**

a. When I'm unhappy, _____ cry.

b. The building caught fire and _____ quickly burned to the ground.

c. Give this apple to Jane. _____ hasn't got one.

d. _____ all went to the movies last Saturday.

e. John and David are cricketers. _____ play for their church team.

f. Donald is sick. _____ has been in bed for a week.

g. 'Will _____ come in for tea?' asked mum.

4 Write the personal pronouns used in 3.

_____

5 Fill in the spaces in these sentences. Choose from these personal pronouns:
me, him, her, it, us, you, them.

a. 'Will you lend ____ that book?' I asked.

b. I'll give it to _____ because they need it.

c. All of _____ would like to go on a holiday.

d. I've got a funny story to tell _____ .

e. My coat was too small so I gave ____ to Peter.

f. Judy was so untidy, I told _____ I couldn't stay overnight.

g. Lawrence is my friend. I'd like to go camping with _____ .

6 Write the personal pronouns used in 5.

_____

7 Find the personal pronouns used in this word maze. You will find them across or down.

8 Write the personal pronouns here.

_____

_____

t	h	e	y	a	l
h	f	r	o	b	r
e	c	d	u	e	i
m	e	s	f	u	s
g	h	h	j	s	i
j	w	e	t	k	l

9 Finish this story. Use these pronouns:
us, they her, she, we, it, them.

CAMPING AT THE BEACH

Our family always goes to the beach for the holidays. _____ get there early to get a good spot for the tent. Dad and Uncle Ron put up the tent and _____ help _____ . _____ takes time to put _____ up well. Once _____ is up, mum moves in and arranges everything. ____ likes doing this and sends dad and Uncle Ron away. I'd help, but she won't ever let anyone help _____ . The Grahams always camp next to ____ .

_____ have three children. The parents don't see a lot of _____ except at meal times.

UNIT 8 — POSSESSIVE PRONOUNS / POSSESSIVE ADJECTIVES

Possessive pronouns stand for nouns and show ownership.

That book is *mine*.

Possessive adjectives also show ownership but are followed by a noun.

My book is on *my* desk.

1 Circle the possessive pronouns and underline the possessive adjectives in this passage.

HOLIDAYS

He always takes his holidays in April. I take mine in July. Mum takes hers in May. The Brady family take theirs in December, before Christmas. When do you take yours?

Last year's holiday was the best ever. I went skiing for the first time. The skiing season is at its height in July. Our Australian skiing season is sometimes shortened by hot weather. The ski resorts only run their chairlifts when there is plenty of snow.

2 Write the possessive pronouns.

_____

3 Write the possessive adjectives.

_____

4 Finish these sentences using these possessive pronouns:
mine, his, hers, its, ours, yours, theirs.

a. 'That parcel is _____,' I said.

b. 'Give it back to _____,' shouted my teacher. 'It's Sarah's.'

c. 'Is this book _____?' I asked Stephen.

d. Fishing is a favourite pastime of _____ . They go fishing every weekend.

e. 'It's _____ . Leave it alone,' they called.

5 Write the possessive pronouns used.

_____

6 Finish these sentences using these possessive adjectives: my, his, her, its, our, your, their.

a. David catches a lot of fish from _____ boat.

b. Everyone was singing. _____ song was 'Advance Australia Fair'.

c. Donna took _____ dress to the dry cleaners.

d. The pony tossed _____ head and kicked up _____ back legs.

e. It's all _____ fault.

f. _____ national flower is wattle blossom.

g. _____ eyes are dim I cannot see.

7 Write the possessive adjectives used.

_____

8 Wiggleword. The clue is the missing word. The missing word is a possessive pronoun or a possessive adjective.

ACROSS

3. She told her teacher that it was _____ .

4. The house had _____ door on the side.

6. I told them it was _____ fault.

7. _____ teacher took us skiing.

9. My parents believed the money was _____ .

DOWN

1. He hung up _____ hat and coat.

2. They own it. It is _____ house.

5. Everything I have is _____ .

8. It is _____ , I tell you.

UNIT 9

GENDER WITH PRONOUNS

Pronouns stand for nouns so you have to look at the nouns they stand for to know their gender.

The gender may be:
- masculine, e.g. he (male)   *He* plays tennis.
- feminine, e.g. she (female)   *She* plays netball.
- neuter, e.g. it (neither male nor female)   *It* is a strong wheelbarrow.
- common, e.g. I (either male or female)   *I* am a doctor.

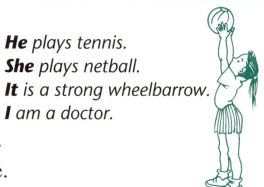

1 Place the underlined pronouns in their correct box.

a. John is five years old. <u>He</u> is tall for his age.

b. Sarah is a clown. <u>She</u> is very funny.

c. Tom drew a sketch of the teacher. It made <u>him</u> look very funny.

d. Captain Matchbox's Whoopee Band made <u>us</u> all laugh.

e. <u>They</u> all came to the fancy dress ball dressed as cats.

f. <u>I</u> like the way <u>you</u> wiggle your nose and ears. Is <u>it</u> hard to do?

g. It is <u>theirs</u>. They have won the prize.

MASCULINE	FEMININE	NEUTER	COMMON
_____	_____	_____	_____
_____	_____	_____	_____
_____	_____	_____	_____
_____	_____	_____	_____

2 Read this passage and circle the pronouns that are feminine gender.

RACHEL'S GAME

Rachel had a favourite game. She used to hide the newspaper every morning. Her parents would ask her to tell them when they were getting close to where she had hidden it. She was good at giving clues. Sometimes the clues were so clever that the newspaper wasn't found. Sometimes Rachel's parents became a bit cross with her. But this never stopped her from doing it again next morning.

3 Arrange these pronouns into their masculine, feminine, neuter or common gender boxes. The pronouns are:
mine, ours, him, its, you, it, anyone, each, herself, she, himself, he, everything.

MASCULINE	FEMININE	NEUTER	COMMON

Indefinite pronouns usually end in -body, -one or -thing. If they end in -body or -one (*somebody, someone*) they will be common gender.

Someone **please turn on the lights.**

If they end in -thing (*anything*), they will be neuter gender.

Anything **could happen.**

4 Cross out the wrong pronouns used in these sentences.

a. (Something, Somebody) laughed loudly.

b. I'd give (anything, anybody) to hear a funny story.

c. Suddenly, (everybody, everything) went black.

d. Does (anything, anybody) have a torch?

e. Don't touch (anyone, anything). (Nobody, Nothing) must be moved.

5 Circle the best pronouns to complete this story.

CIRCUS FUN

(We, Us) all went to the circus last week. Dad said (he, she) liked the lion tamer. My mum said (he, she) liked the elephants. My sister Penny said (she, her, him) liked the ponies. But (I, me) liked the clowns.

'Why did (you, I) like the clowns, David?' asked Penny.

'Because (they, them) made (I, me) laugh,' (he, I, him) said.

'David's a bit of a clown,' said Penny. That's why (he, she) likes them.'

'Do you like horses because you look like (them, us)?' David asked Penny.

UNIT 10 — PRONOUNS / VERBS AGREE IN NUMBER

**Number refers to singular or plural.
A singular pronoun takes a singular verb.**

He sings **funny songs.** (*He — sings*)

A plural pronoun takes a plural verb.

They sing **funny songs.** (*They — sing*)

1 Circle the correct words to finish these sentences.

a. They all (is, are) dressing up for the ball.

b. She (looks, look) very funny in that hat.

c. I (am, are) in the school band.

d. Their books (was, were) left outside.

e. I will (go, goes) by myself.

f. Ours (is, are) the funniest costumes.

g. Will his parents (goes, go) to the show?

**2 Use these words to finish these sentences:
he, she, it me, mine, I, you, they.**

a. _____ was sick yesterday.

b. _____ will go to the circus next Saturday.

c. _____ have a new TV at home.

d. The movie was very old but _____ was very funny.

e. My dog can do a lot of tricks. _____ can stand up on his hind legs.

f. The circus is coming to town. _____ will be here next week.

g. Those buildings are very old. _____ will have to be pulled down.

h. That joke book is _____ .

i. _____ am coming over by myself.

j. John, are _____ going to sing tonight?

3 Put a tick in the box if correct and a cross if wrong. The first one is done for you.

a. she sings ✓
b. we is
c. they have
d. you is
e. it were

f. I am
g. we had
h. this are
i. those were
j. everyone is

4 What is happening?

a. She _____ .

b. He _____ .

c. They _____ .

d. I _____ .

e. You _____ .

f. It _____ .

5 Fill in the missing words. Use these words:
its, was, I, saw, it.

A FUNNY STORY

One day _____ was riding my bike home from school. I _____ a big dog chasing a cat. The cat _____ headed for a hole in the fence.

When _____ reached there, _____ slipped through the hole. The big dog couldn't stop in time and got _____ head stuck in the hole. _____ twisted and scratched and barked but _____ couldn't get _____ head out. The cat sat on the top of the step and licked _____ fur.

UNIT 11 VISITS
DESCRIPTIVE ADJECTIVES

Descriptive adjectives **tell us more about a person or thing.**

For example, in the phrase,

an *exciting* visit

exciting is a descriptive adjective.
It tells us more about the visit.

1 Underline the descriptive adjectives in this passage, then write them in the spaces. The first one is done for you.

AN EXCITING VISIT

I like to visit our young neighbours. We play noisy games on the back lawn. Then we eat juicy oranges from the old tree growing near the paling fence. Afterwards we watch exciting shows on the television in the spare bedroom with the blue wallpaper.

young _____

_____

2 Think of some adjectives to describe a visit. One visit is exciting, another is boring. Write the adjectives in the space below.

a. **exciting:** _____

b. **boring:** _____

3 Fill in the spaces with descriptive adjectives. Pick the words from the bag.

My _____ friend lives on a _____ farm near a _____ river. I go there during the _____ holidays in a _____ train. We have a _____ time.

big   passenger
great   school
best   deep

4 Write in another adjective. Pick from the tour bus.

big, _____ oranges
fat, _____ boys
kind, _____ uncles
_____ , healthy athletes
deep, _____ river
wonderful, _____ visit
_____ , white swan

Tour bus words: leafy muddy long old juicy fit beautiful lazy noisy exciting

_____ , freight train
_____ , busy classroom
tall, _____ tree

Adjectives can come after their nouns in a sentence.

The boys are *noisy*.

5 Underline the adjectives in these sentences.

a. The visit was long and exciting.
b. Our bus was crowded and slow.
c. The lunch was delicious and nutritious.
d. She is clever, caring and kind.
e. This is easy and that is hard.

6 Make your own adjectives. Write them in the spaces beside the nouns. The first one is done for you.

care   **careful**   health   _____
happiness   _____   fun   _____
warmth   _____   hunger   _____
peace   _____   fitness   _____
music   _____   excitement _____

7 Make adjectives from the nouns in brackets. Write them in the spaces.

We went on a (length) _____ excursion. Our (kindness) _____ teacher took us. It was (heat) _____ in the (crowd) _____ bus. I ate my (juice) _____ apple on the way.

UNIT 12 VISITS: DEGREE WITH REGULAR ADJECTIVES

Adjectives have *degree*. They can show more or less of a thing.

The three words, *strong*, *stronger* and *strongest* show degree.
- Someone is *strong*.
- Someone else is *stronger*.
- Someone else is *strongest*.

strong   stronger   strongest

The three levels of degree are positive, comparative and superlative.

1 Fill in the comparative and superlative degree for each adjective. The first one is done for you.

Positive	Comparative	Superlative
strong	stronger	strongest
long	_____	_____
happy	_____	_____
fast	_____	_____
slow	_____	_____
green	_____	_____
small	_____	_____
big	_____	_____
tall	_____	_____
old	_____	_____

> You use the comparative when two things are compared;
> you use the superlative when three or more are compared.

the *bigger* of the two   the *biggest* of the three

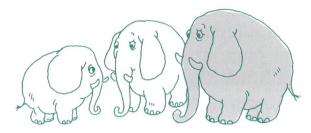

2 Cross out the incorrect words in the brackets.

a. I am the (big, bigger, biggest) boy in my class, but he is the (big, bigger, biggest) of the two boys in our family.

b. It is the (fast, faster, fastest) ship in the whole navy, but it is the (slow, slower, slowest) of the two battleships in big seas.

c. What is the (easy, easier, easiest) way to get there out of these three?

d. What is the (easy, easier, easiest) way out of these two?

3 Write in the correct adjectives. Make them from the words in brackets.

a. the (easy) _____ of the two exams.
b. the (hard) _____ of the three apples.
c. the (funny) _____ of the two films.
d. the (tall) _____ of the two brothers.
e. the (fat) _____ of the ten chickens.

4 Fill in the spaces with the adjectives in the positive, comparative or superlative degree.

POSITIVE	COMPARATIVE	SUPERLATIVE
_____	finer	_____
_____	_____	prettiest
_____	richer	_____
sharp	_____	_____
young	_____	_____

UNIT 13 — DEGREE WITH IRREGULAR ADJECTIVES

Some adjectives sound awkward if you add 'er' and 'est'. These are usually longer words, like the word *beautiful*. You would not say 'beautifuller' or 'beautifullest'.

You would say *more beautiful* and *most beautiful*. That is, you would add the adverb *more* or *most* to form the comparative or superlative.

1 Fill in the comparative and superlative degree of these adjectives. The first one is done for you.

Positive	Comparative	Superlative
beautiful	more beautiful	most beautiful
horrible		
crooked		
reliable		
terrible		
brilliant		

2 Finish this table. Some of the adjectives are regular; some are not.

Positive	Comparative	Superlative
hot		
sunny		
changeable		
early		
careful		
courageous		

Other adjectives are even more irregular. They change the whole word in the comparative or superlative. The adjective, *good*, is an example. The three degrees are *good*, *better* and *best*.

3 Finish this table of irregular adjectives. The first one is done for you.

Positive	Comparative	Superlative
good	better	best
many	more	
little		least
bad	worse	

4 Cross out the incorrect adjectives in this passage.

A VISIT TO THE MOUNTAINS

It was the (good, better, best) visit we have made. I've never had a (good, better, best) time. Although it was a (cold, colder, coldest) winter, it was much (cold, colder, coldest) last year. We climbed some of the (beautiful, more beautiful, most beautiful) mountains I have ever seen.

5 Write a sentence for each of these adjectives: **best, louder, less, wettest, more reliable.**

a. _____
b. _____
c. _____
d. _____
e. _____

UNIT 14 · VISITS: ADJECTIVES FOR NOUNS AND PRONOUNS

Writing the best adjectives to describe nouns and pronouns is important. If you visited a sports carnival, you would see many athletes running and jumping.

Here are some adjectives to describe them. You could probably think of many more.

FIT   FAST   SLIM   STRONG   SPEEDY   TRAINED
HEALTHY   DETERMINED   COMPETITIVE   MUSCULAR

1 Write down two or more adjectives to describe each of these things you might see on a visit.

a. mountain _____
b. river _____
c. beach _____
d. people in town _____
e. fish in an aquarium _____

2 Write adjectives in the spaces.

a. _____ _____ footballer
b. _____ _____ ballet dancer
c. _____ _____ teacher
d. _____ _____ tennis player
e. _____ _____ puppy
f. _____ _____ parrot
g. _____ _____ fire engine

3 A VISIT TO THE ZOO

Imagine you made a visit to a zoo. Write down two adjectives to describe each bird or animal in the pictures. Write them in the spaces. Draw a line from the adjectives to the pictures in each case.

_____

_____

_____

_____

_____

_____

_____

4
Finish these sentences with adjectives to describe these animals and birds. You may use some of the adjectives from Exercise 1.

a. The lion is _____ and _____ .

b. The giraffe is _____ and _____ .

c. The monkey is _____ and _____ .

d. The parrots are _____ and _____ .

5 Fill in the spaces with descriptive adjectives.

A VISIT TO THE FIRE STATION

The fire engine was _____ in colour and had _____ ladders on the top and _____ hoses on the side. The fire fighters wore _____ helmets and _____ _____ boots.

6 Write adjectives to describe these things.

_____ skyscraper   _____ ocean

_____ cat   _____ blind mice

_____ story   _____ rose

_____ grass   _____ old owl

7 Write adjectives which are the opposites of these words.

fat _____   light _____   good _____   hot _____

low _____   soft _____   quick _____   sweet _____

UNIT 15 VISITS — RECOGNISING VERBS

Verbs **are doing, having or being words.**

1 Circle the verbs in these sentences. The first is done for you.

a. I (visited) my grandma last Saturday.
b. We go to Yass on the train.
c. Dad has two aunts in the country.
d. They are now very old.
e. The class went on an excursion to the zoo.
f. The animals looked very lazy.
g. The lions were the laziest.
h. The monkeys were playing chasings.
i. They were having a good time.
j. We had lunch at the zoo.

2 Write the verbs.

_____
_____

3 Circle the verbs in these questions.

a. Is this the last train?
b. Has grandma a spare bed?
c. Who missed the ferry?
d. Were John and Judy going to the zoo?
e. What has happened to Sarah?

4 Write the verbs.

_____
_____

5 Use these verbs to finish these sentences: **is going, looked, went, was, has gone**.

a. We _____ to the Gold Coast for a holiday.

b. John _____ in his bag for his ticket.

c. Sarah _____ almost too sick to come.

d. Where _____ David _____ this weekend?

e. Who _____ to town tomorrow?

6 We often use verbs in contractions: *I have—I've*. Here are some contractions. Write down the full form and circle the verbs. The first one is done for you.

a. I've   I (have)   f. she's   _____

b. we'd   _____   g. there's   _____

c. they've _____   h. I'd   _____

d. it's   _____   i. we've   _____

e. you're _____   j. they'll   _____

7 Read this poem and circle the verbs. Don't miss the verbs in the contractions.

WHEN I VISIT MY COUSIN

When I visit my cousin,
I always have fun;
We play many games,
And run in the sun.
Or we sit very quietly,
Beside a big fire;
And look at the tele,
Or the cross on the spire,
Of the church of St Mary's,
That's just up the hill;

It's all very peaceful,
It's all very still.
And sometimes I stay,
For more than a week;
There's plenty to do,
And plenty to eat,
And plenty of time,
To have our first fight;
Then I want to go home,
That very same night.

Gregory Blaxell

8 Write the verbs.

_____

_____

UNIT 16

TENSE IN SIMPLE VERBS

Tense refers to time and tells us whether the process or action is taking place now (*present tense*), has taken place (*past tense*) or will take place some time in the future (*future tense*).

1 Fill in the blanks in these sentences with verbs in the present tense. Use these verbs:
am, buys, climbs, goes, grow, plants, phones, scratches, swim, weeds.
The first is done for you.

a. I **grow** tomatoes and lettuce.

b. Dad _____ the garden for Mum.

c. I _____ for a swimming club.

d. Rachel _____ that big tree very easily.

e. Mum _____ her friend Ailsa every day.

f. He _____ to the nursery every Saturday.

g. My sister _____ a ticket every Sunday.

h. My dog _____ all the time.

i. Our teacher _____ trees in our playground.

j. I _____ a gardener.

2 Fill in this table using verbs in the present tense. The first one is done for you.

I am	he **is**	they **are**
I buy	she _____	you _____
I _____	she climbs	we _____
I _____	it goes	they _____
I grow	she _____	you _____
I _____	he plants	we _____
I _____	she phones	they _____
I _____	he scratches	you _____
I swim	she _____	we _____
I _____	he weeds	they _____

36

PGH 27

Verbs in the past tense usually end in 'ed'. This is sometimes shortened to 'd' or 't'. Some verbs change their spelling in the past tense, e.g. *swim—swam* (not 'swimmed'). The verbs that do this are known as strong or irregular verbs.

3 Fill in the blanks in these sentences with verbs in the past tense. Use these verbs: **broomed, dug, had, helped, hosed, mowed, planted, raked, was, washed.**

a. Dad _____ a new garden.
b. He _____ the garden to make it smooth.
c. Mum _____ some beans.
d. I _____ mum.
e. My sister Jill _____ the family car.
f. My brother John _____ the lawn.
g. Mum _____ up the leaves in the driveway.
h. She then _____ the garden because it was very dry.
i. The family _____ a day in the garden.
j. It _____ hard work but fun.

4 Fill in the blanks in these sentences with verbs in the future tense. Use these words: **will be, will get, will grow, will have, will help, will plant.**

a. Next year, dad _____ _____ some carrots and peas.
b. They _____ _____ the best vegies ever grown.
c. The family _____ _____ enough to give some to our friends.
d. Your family _____ _____ some for sure.
e. Next week, mum _____ _____ some more seedlings.
f. Dad _____ _____ her plant them.

5 The future tense uses *shall* or *will* which are often written as a contraction. Write down the contracted forms. The first one is done for you.

a. I shall   **I'll**
b. he will   _____
c. she will   _____
d. it will   _____
e. we shall   _____
f. you will   _____
g. they will   _____

37

UNIT 17 — GROWING THINGS
PRESENT AND PAST PARTICIPLES

Present Participles

Present participles end in 'ing' and are used with helping verbs to show action going on.

I am *digging* in the garden.

1 Circle the present participles in these sentences. Write them below.

a. I am studying how plants grow.
b. I was planting some cabbages when you arrived.
c. They were trying hard but they have poor soil.
d. You will be digging your potatoes soon, I suppose.
e. He was beginning to show an interest in the garden.
f. I'll be using a rotary hoe in future.

_____

_____

2 Underline the helping verbs in the sentences above. Write them below.

_____

_____

3 Write the present participles of these verbs. Remember your spelling rules. The first one is done for you.

a. (to) dig   **digging**   f. (to) wash   _____
b. (to) plant   _____   g. (to) fix   _____
c. (to) rake   _____   h. (to) want   _____
d. (to) carry   _____   i. (to) go   _____
e. (to) fold   _____   j. (to) use   _____

38

PGH 25

4 Write sentences using these verbs.

a. **am going**: _____

b. **was spreading**: _____

c. **will be sending**: _____

Past Participles

> Past participles usually end in 'ed' which is sometimes shortened to 'd' or 't'. Past participles are used with the helping verb 'to have' to show action that has stopped.

He has *stopped* to see the garden.

5 Circle the past participles in these sentences. Write them below.

a. We have travelled more than 500 km.
b. They had completed their journey when it happened.
c. You will have commenced school by February.
d. It has happened that way before.
e. She had arrived early.
f. He will have worked very hard for the last six months.

_____

6 Underline the helping verbs in the sentences above and write them below.

_____

7 Write the past participle of these verbs. Remember your spelling rules. The first one is done for you.

a. (to) plant   has **planted**   f. (to) fix   will have _____
b. (to) rake   had _____   g. (to) want   has _____
c. (to) carry   will have _____   h. (to) use   had _____
d. (to) fold   have _____   i. (to) mow   will have _____
e. (to) wash   had _____   j. (to) water   have _____
                                                                            k. (to) store   had _____

UNIT 18 — GROWING THINGS
PAST PARTICIPLES OF STRONG VERBS

Some verbs change their spelling in the past tense and the past participle. These are the strong verbs.

INFINITIVE	PAST TENSE	PAST PARTICIPLE
(to) ring	rang	(has) rung

All past participles have helping verbs.
Many strong verbs have 'n' or 'en' endings in the past participle.

INFINITIVE	PAST TENSE	PAST PARTICIPLE
(to) bite	bit	(has) bitten

1 Complete this table. The first one is done for you.

INFINITIVE	PAST TENSE	PAST PARTCIPLE
a. (to) break	broke	has **broken**
b. (to) drive	drove	has _____
c. (to) fly	flew	has _____
d. (to) give	gave	has _____
e. (to) ride	rode	has _____
f. (to) steal	stole	has _____
g. (to) take	took	has _____
h. (to) throw	threw	has _____
i. (to) wear	wore	has _____
j. (to) write	wrote	has _____

2 Circle the past participles in these sentences.

a. I have given grandma a large cabbage.

b. They had fallen off the truck.

c. You have ridden for many kilometres.

d. It has taken five years of hard work.

e. I have written Jimmy a long letter.

3 Underline the helping verbs in the sentences above.

Often strong verbs have lost their 'en' or 'n' ending in the past participle. However many of them have the same form of the verb for the past tense as for the past participle.

INFINITIVE	PAST TENSE	PAST PARTICIPLE
(to) become	became	has become

4 Complete this table. The first one is done for you.

INFINITIVE	PAST TENSE	PAST PARTCIPLE
a. (to) begin	began	has **begun**
b. (to) dig	dug	has _____
c. (to) ring	rang	has _____
d. (to) sit	sat	has _____
e. (to) stand	stood	has _____
f. (to) swim	swam	has _____
g. (to) win	won	has _____
h. (to) wind	wound	has _____

5 Circle the past participles in these sentences.

a. She has dug a hole for the new tree.

b. They had sung a song for Spring.

c. I will have swum a kilometre in training.

d. You have won many prizes for your vegies.

e. We had found a spider's hole in the garden.

6 Underline the helping verbs in the sentences above.

7 Complete these sentences using these past participles:
begun, flown, frozen, spun, taken.

a. David and Sarah have _____ to England on a Qantas flight.

b. I have not _____ my medicine.

c. The orb spider has _____ a beautiful web.

d. Harvesting has _____ .

e. The water in this dish had _____ .

UNIT 19 — GROWING THINGS: FINDING ADVERBS

Adverbs add meaning to verbs, adjectives and other adverbs.

For example, *slowly* is an adverb in this sentence:

Trees grow *slowly*.

1 Underline the adverbs in this passage, then write them in the spaces. The first one is done for you.

TREES GROW <u>SLOWLY</u>

Some things grow quickly; some things grow slowly. Vegetables grow quickly, if you water them regularly and carefully.

But trees grow gradually over many years.

slowly _____

_____

The word *very* is an adverb in this sentence.

It has *very* green leaves.

2 Underline the adverbs in this passage then write them in the spaces. The first one is done for you.

<u>VERY</u> GREEN LEAVES

This tree has very green leaves which are extremely large. The nectar of the brightly coloured flowers is the most popular food of the constantly hungry parrots.

very _____

_____

_____

_____

The word *too* is an adverb in this sentence.

Don't eat *too* quickly.

3 Underline the adverbs in this passage. The first one is done for you.

GROWING TOO QUICKLY AND TOO SLOWLY

If plants grow too quickly they can become diseased. If they grow very slowly they may become completely stunted. You need to help them to grow at the right pace. Water them regularly and fertilise them well.

4 Write an adverb in each space.

a. Tom walks _____ and Jenny walks _____ .

b. That tree is _____ tall.

c. The garden has had _____ much water.

d. The grass is _____ long and _____ dry.

e. 'This is the _____ expensive plant in the shop,' said the man _____ .

f. I dug _____ around the roots of the plant.

g. Vegetables should be cooked _____ .

5 Write adverbs from the box to fill the spaces.

_____ tall tree

_____ many apples

Run _____ .

Chew _____ .

_____ exhausted

_____ written

Box: too, very, carefully, slowly, completely, quickly

43

Unit 20 — TYPES OF ADVERBS

GROWING THINGS

Adverbs tell how, when, where and why.

I ran *quickly*.   (*Quickly* **tells** *how* **I ran**.)
I will go *tomorrow*.   (*Tomorrow* **tells** *when* **I will go**.)
They went *there*.   (*There* **tells** *where* **they went**.)
Why are you coming?   (*Why* **asks** *why* **you are coming**.)

1 Write the underlined adverbs in the spaces, then write if they tell *how, where, when* or *why*. **The first one is done for you.**

THE ATHLETE

Trees grow <u>slowly</u>;
Grass grows <u>fast</u>.
I run <u>slowly</u>,
And I come <u>last</u>.

Gordon Winch

     slowly   how
_____ _____
_____ _____
_____ _____

HELPING MUM

'I'll do it <u>tomorrow</u>.
I promise,' I say.
'You won't,' says my mother.
'You'll do it <u>today</u>!'

Gordon Winch

_____ _____
_____ _____

MY NEW BIKE

Put it <u>there</u> near the tele;
Put it <u>here</u> if you like,
But don't scratch the paint
On my shiny, new bike.

Gordon Winch

_____ _____
_____ _____

ROUGH ROSE

<u>Why</u> did you hit him?
<u>Why</u> did you, Rose?
<u>Why</u> did you punch him,
<u>Right</u> on the nose.

Gordon Winch

_____ _____
_____ _____
_____ _____
_____ _____

2 Write adverbs in the spaces. Pick from the box. The type of adverb is in brackets. The first one is done for you.

a. Tom is growing (how) __quickly__ .
b. Jill came (where) _____ in the race.
c. I will see you (when) _____ .
d. Plant the trees (where) _____ .
e. (Why) _____ did you call out?
f. I would like my breakfast (when) _____ .
g. Come (place) _____ at once.
h. Think (how) _____ before you answer.
i. Cut the lawn (time) _____ .
j. (Why) _____ are the leaves so green?

```
tomorrow
here
early
why
now
first
why
there
carefully
```

3 Write a sentence for each of these adverbs. The first one is done for you:
here, later, tomorrow, why, easily, happily.

a. __Come here!__
b. _____
c. _____
d. _____
e. _____
f. _____

4 ADVERB WIGGLEWORD

Across

1. Opposite of slowly (how)
3. Not here but _____ (where)
4. Very frequently (when)
7. Very slow (how)
8. The day before today (when)
9. Asks a question (why)

Down

2. With great care (how)
5. This very minute (when)
6. The day after today (when)
8. Every year (when)

21 UNIT SPORT — FINDING PREPOSITIONS

Prepositions are found in front of nouns or pronouns.

in the pool
PREPOSITION — NOUN

near us
PREPOSITION — PRONOUN

They are often little words: *in, on, to, up* and *into* are prepositions. There are many others.

1 Underline the prepositions and put a box around the nouns that go with them. The first one is done for you.

a. I stood <u>near</u> the [captain].

b. I swam in the sea.

c. I rode on the bike.

d. I walked to the oval.

e. I ran up the hill.

f. I went into the gym.

2 Underline the prepositions and put a box around the pronouns that go with them. The first one is done for you.

a. They divided the oranges <u>amongst</u> [us].

b. We made a circle around them.

c. I could see the river beneath me.

d. They ran after us.

e. Give the baton to her.

f. Take the ball from him.

The word *preposition* means 'placed in front'. That is why you find prepositions in front of nouns or pronouns.

3 Fill in the gaps with prepositions. Choose them from the box.

a. I play tennis _____ the new court _____ our place. I practise hitting the ball _____ the net _____ my friend. Would you like to play tennis _____ me?

b. We swim _____ the pool _____ the beach. If we go _____ the surf, we swim _____ the flags; not _____ them.

on, in, near, over, between, outside, with, to, into, at

46

> **WATCH OUT FOR ADVERBS.**
> **If words like 'past' or 'after' do not have a noun or pronoun following them, they are adverbs, not prepositions.**

I walked *past* the shop.   (PREPOSITION)
I walked *past*.   (ADVERB)

4 Underline the prepositions in these sentences. Draw boxes around the adverbs that look like prepositions.

a. Did you see the other runners go past? They went across the finishing line after the winner.

b. Cross over. There may be cars coming along the road in a minute.

c. Jump up! Over the counter. That's it!

d. Jack and Jill went up the hill. Then they fell down.

e. Don't pour the water down the drain; pour it on the garden.

f. Jump on! The bus is leaving and it will not go past your house.

5 Find the prepositions in this box of letters. Read across and down. Write the prepositions in the space.

f	w	i	t	h	a	a
r	i	n	t	o	t	c
o	t	s	k	l	q	r
m	h	i	d	u	o	o
r	i	d	o	w	n	s
p	n	e	a	r	t	s
a	f	t	e	r	o	w

_____

_____

_____

UNIT 22 SPORT: USING PREPOSITIONS

Let's practise using prepositions.

1 Fill in the spaces with prepositions.

in, on, down

a. Running _____ races is fun. Riding _____ a horse is too. But I like rafting _____ a river.

across, under

b. The boat sailed _____ the ocean. The sailing ship sailed _____ the bridge.

before, during, after

c. You should warm up _____ a game. _____ a game, you should play hard. _____ a game you can have an orange and a rest.

onto, into

d. The team ran _____ the field. The swimmer dived _____ the water.

around, beside

e. Let's run _____ the oval. You can run _____ me.

to, from

f. My socks are similar ____ yours. Your sweater is different _____ mine.

2 Use prepositions from the examples above to complete these sentences.

_____ a game I try my hardest. I try to play well from the moment I run _____ the field. Before playing I run _____ the oval to warm up. Last week we played the leaders. Their shorts were similar _____ ours but the colour of their sweaters was different _____ the red of ours.

48

3 Some prepositions have opposites such as *up* and *down*. Write the opposites in the spaces.

a. She went *inside* the house.
   I stayed _____ the house.

b. The big dog jumped *over* the fence.
   The little dog ran _____ the fence.

c. He sat *on* the horse.
   I fell _____ the horse.

d. The sky is *above* us.
   The ground is _____ us.

e. My sister is *like* me.
   My brother is _____ me.

4 Fill in the gaps with prepositions from the box.

| To | up | Along | into | on | Beside | into | Across | beneath | in |

a. Jack and Jill
   Went ____ the hill.

b. Humpty Dumpty
   Sat ____ a wall.

c. _____ the mighty ocean
   _____ the winding road
   The ships and trucks will carry
   Their vast and heavy load.

d. _____ the lake,
   _____ the trees,
   Fluttering and dancing
   ____ the breeze.

e. Throw the ball
   _____ the net;
   Jump _____ the pool;
   Grab your books and hat and lunch,
   Then hurry off _____ school.

5 Some words take special prepositions:
listen to, agree with, take from, give to, and **different from**.
Write three sentences with the following special words in them.

a. **listen to:** _____

b. **agree with:** _____

c. **different from:** _____

49

UNIT 23 — SPORT

PREPOSITIONS AND PRONOUNS

In this unit, we will practise writing the correct personal pronouns after prepositions. Here is a list of personal pronouns which follow prepositions. They are said to be in the *objective case*.
All you have to do is choose the correct one. In most cases they just sound right.

	PERSONAL PRONOUNS OBJECTIVE CASE		
SINGULAR	me	you	him, her, it
PLURAL	us	you	them

1 Write in the correct pronoun after each preposition.

a. That book belongs to Mary. Give it to _____ .

b. The Smith family are going on holidays. They are taking me with _____ .

c. Jill is going, too. I will go with _____ .

d. We are next. You can go after _____ .

e. You are catching the bus. May I go with _____ ?

f. Ali and Kim have one apple. We will divide it between _____ .

Take special care when there are two pronouns after a preposition. They must *both* be in the objective case.

2 Write in the correct pronouns after each preposition.

a. Tim and I won prizes at the sports day. They were given to _____ and _____ .

b. Mary and Jim bought a watermelon. It was divided between _____ and _____ .

c. The Flynns are going to the cricket, and so are we. You may come with _____ or _____ .

3 Cross out the incorrect pronouns.

a. That bat is mine. Give it to (her, me).

b. When we won the race, the spectators gathered around (us, them).

c. Dad and I like swimming. Would you like to come swimming with (him, them) and (us, me)?

d. That's our ball. Don't take it from (them, us).

e. Carol and Peter are over there. Let's go and sit with (us, her) and (him, her).

f. Come over to play, Tom, and bring your basketball with (her, he, you).

4 Do this Correct Pronoun Wordpuzzle.

ACROSS

2. You need a ball, and a bat with _____ .

4. We own it; it belongs to _____ .

5. Jack fell down the hill and Jill came tumbling after _____ .

6. Bill and Sue have one banana. Divide it between him and _____ .

7. I'm running in the race. You can run with _____ .

DOWN

1. You're next; I'll go after _____ .

3. They went and we went with _____ .

5 Finish these sentences with pronouns. Use as many different ones as you can.

a. Give the book to _____ .

b. Come to the game with _____ and _____ .

c. Divide the melon between _____ and _____ .

d. I want to sit near _____ .

e. Keep the score for _____ and _____ .

Unit 24 — SPORT: RECOGNISING CONJUNCTIONS

Co-ordinate Conjunctions

Co-ordinate conjunctions **join words, groups of words, or sentences.**

> She was wet *and* tired.
> They wandered across the hills *but* not across the desert.
> This is her book *and* she can have it.

1 Circle the co-ordinate conjunctions in these sentences.

a. He was strong and fast when playing soccer.
b. She is tall and thin and a good netball player.
c. He passed the ball to the left but never to the right.
d. He has to play well today or he'll be dropped.
e. She was very tired yet she kept swimming.

2 Join these words, groups of words or sentences with a co-ordinate conjunction. Choose from these: **and, but, for, nor, or, so, yet.**

a. Jack _____ Jill
b. over the hills _____ far away
c. He has a cat. He does not have a dog.
   _____
d. Do you want to play netball _____ teeball?
e. I didn't bring my sports shoes. I did bring my sports socks.
   _____

Correlative Conjunctions

> **Some conjunctions go in pairs.**
>
> as ... as

> These are called *correlative conjunctions*.

WRITE WELL 3 ANSWERS

UNIT 1
1. nose, rose, teeth, pie, ear, eye, skin, feet, lip, tongue
2. sister, cousin, uncle, aunt, grandmother, grandfather

UNIT 2
1. a. b. c. See 2
2. **Common**: beach, holidays, cousin, year, parents, top, mother, father, tent, damper, ranger
   Proper: Jane, Mollymook, Mt Kosciusko, Christmas, Bill, Ali, Kakadu National Park, Joe Drake, Holden
6. **Days**: Monday, Tuesday, Wednesday, Thursday, Friday, Saturday, Sunday
   Months: January, February, August, November, December
   Special Days: Australia Day, Anzac Day, Christmas Day

UNIT 3
1. a. litter
   b. team
   c. swarm
   d. herd
   e. bunch
2. birds/sheep, fish, singers
3. team, bunch, litter, crowd
4. kindness, greed, anger, sadness truth, love
5. a. happiness
   b. anger
   c. kindness
   d. truth
   e. sadness

UNIT 4
1. tents, cars, beaches, babies, men
2. sandwiches, potatoes, tents, knives, loaves
3. lady, woman, tomato, spoonful, chief, bee, sheep, mouse, story, ferry
4. **Across**:
   2. watches
   3. babies
   4. loaves
   6. herds
   7. wolves
   Down:
   1. schools
   2. wives
   3. beaches
   5. foxes
   6. hearts
5. tomatoes, bushes, foxes, potatoes, beaches, catches
   ....
   babies, bodies, stories, berries, fairies, ferries
   ....
   journeys, cliffs, waves, heights, pianos, valleys
   ....
   wolves, leaves, wives, knives, loaves, thieves

UNIT 5
1. **Masculine**: Angus, Steve, father, men
   Feminine: Jennifer, Noni, mother, women
   Neuter: zoo, hamburgers, lunch, ferry, waves, rocks, shore
2. boy M, bicycle N, queen F, king M, campfire N, cow, F, bull M, rope N, ram M, potato N, rock N, tent N, duck F, girl F, bone N, niece F, actor M or F, grandfather M, aunt F, ewe F
3. boy/girl, king/queen, tiger/tigress, grandfather/grandmother, nephew/niece, uncle/aunt, prince/princess, drake/duck, gentleman/woman/lady, brother/sister
4. Father M, mother F, Sister F, brother M, Uncle M, Jim, M, Nephew M, niece F, Aunt F, Denise F, Cousins M or F, Jim M, Sue F
   ....
   M-5, F-5
5. a. children
   b. doctor, patients
   c. writer
   d. animals
   e. class, people
   f. cattle, sheep, chickens

UNIT 6
1. Cross out:
   a. is
   b. were
   c. plays
   d. are
   e. were
2. a. are
   b. is
   c. were
   d. has
   e. were, was
3. Cross out:
   a. is
   b. was
   c. is
   d. plays
   e. is
4. a. run
   b. go
   c. were, were
   d. have
5. a. were
   b. They
   c. Tubby Smith
   d. train
   e. have

UNIT 7
1. See 2
2. I, They, I, I, He, He, him, She, they, They, they, We, it, You
3. a. I
   b. it
   c. She
   d. We
   e. They
   f. He
   g. you
4. See 3
5. a. him/her
   b. them
   c. us
   d. you
   e. it
   f. her
   g. him
6. See 5
8. they, them you, me, she, us, he, we
9. We, We, them, It, it, it, She, her, us, They, us

UNIT 8
1. See 2 and 3
2. mine, hers, theirs, yours
3. his, its, our, their
4. a. mine
   b. her
   c. yours
   d. theirs
   e. his/hers/theirs
5. See 4
6. a. his
   b. Their
   c. her
   d. its, its
   e. your
   f. Our
   g. My
7. See 6
8. **Across**:
   3. hers
   4. its
   6. my
   7. Our
   9. theirs
   Down:
   1. his
   2. their
   5. yours
   8. mine

UNIT 9
1. **Masculine**: He, him
   Feminine: She
   Neuter: it, It
   Common: us, They, I, you, theirs
2. See tag
3. **Masculine**: him, himself, he
   Feminine: herself, she
   Neuter: its, it, everything
   Common: mine, ours, you, anyone, each
4. **Cross out**:
   a. Something
   b. anybody
   c. everybody
   d. anything
   e. anyone, Nobody
5. **Circled pronouns are**:
   We, he, she, she, I, you, they, me, I, he, them

UNIT 10
1. a. are
   b. looks
   c. am
   d. were
   e. go
   f. are
   g. go
2. a. I, He, She
   b. I, he, She, They
   c. I, They
   d. it
   e. It, He, She
   f. It
   g. They
   h. mine
   i. I
   j. you
3. a. (✔)
   b. (✘)
   c. (✔)
   d. (✘)
   e. (✘)
   f. (✔)
   g. (✔)
   h. (✘)
   i. (✔)
   j. (✔)
4. a. She is singing.
   b. He is jumping.
   c. They are clapping.
   d. I am fishing
   e. You are reading.
   f. It is cutting.
5. I, saw, was, it, it, its, It, It, it, its, its

UNIT 11
1. young, noisy, back, juicy, old, paling, exciting, spare, blue
3. best/school, big, deep, school, passenger, great
4. juicy
   lazy
   old
   fit
   muddy
   long/exciting
   beautiful
   noisy/long
   exciting
   leafy
5. a. long, exciting
   b. crowded, slow
   c. delicious, nutritious
   d. clever, caring, kind
   e. easy, hard
6. careful, happy, warm peaceful, musical, healthy funny, hungry, fit, exciting
7. lengthy/long, kind, hot, crowded, juicy

UNIT 12
1. **Comparative Superlative**
   stronger   strongest
   longer   longest
   happier   happiest
   faster   fastest
   slower   slowest
   greener   greenest
   smaller   smallest
   bigger   biggest
   taller   tallest
   older   oldest
2. **Cross out**:
   a. big, bigger: big, biggest
   b. fast, faster: slow, slowest
   c. easy, easier
   d. easy, easiest
3. a. easier
   b. hardest
   c. funnier
   d. taller
   e. fattest
4. **Pos Comp Super**
   fine   finer   finest
   pretty prettier prettiest
   rich   richer   richest
   sharp   sharper sharpest
   young   younger youngest

UNIT 13
1. **Comparative**
   more horrible
   more crooked
   more reliable
   more terrible
   more brilliant
   Superlative
   most horrible
   most crooked
   most reliable
   most terrible
   most brilliant
2. **Comparative**
   hotter
   sunnier
   more changeable
   earlier
   more careful
   more courageous
   Superlative
   hottest
   sunniest
   most changeable

WRITE WELL 3 ANSWERS

earliest
most careful
most courageous
3. many, more, most
   little, less, least
   bad, worse, worst
4. **Cross out**:
   good, better: good, best:
   colder, coldest: cold, coldest:
   beautiful, more beautiful

UNIT 14

7. fat-thin, light-dark, good-bad,
   hot-cold, low-high, soft-hard,
   quick-slow, sweet-sour

UNIT 15

1. See 2
2. visited, go, has, are, went,
   looked, were, were playing,
   were having, had
3. See 4
4. Is, Has, missed, Were … going,
   has happened
5. a. went
   b. looked
   c. was
   d. has gone
   e. is going
6. a. I have
   b. we had
   c. they have
   d. it is
   e. you are
   f. she is
   g. there is
   h. I had
   i. we have
   j. they will
7. See 8
8. visit, have, play, run, sit,
   look, is, is, stay, is, want

UNIT 16

1. a. grow
   b. weeds
   c. swim
   d. climbs
   e. phones
   f. goes
   g. buys
   h. scratches
   i. plants
   j. am
2. she buys, you buy,
   I climb, we climb,
   I go, they go,
   she grows, you grow,
   I plant, we plant,
   I phone, they phone,
   I scratch, you scratch,
   she swims, we swim,
   I weed, they weed
3. a. dug
   b. raked
   c. planted
   d. helped
   e. washed/hosed
   f. mowed
   g. broomed
   h. hosed
   i. had
   j. was
4. a. will plant/will grow
   b. will be
   c. will have/will get
   d. will get
   e. will plant
   f. will help
5. a. I'll
   b. he'll
   c. she'll
   d. it'll
   e. we'll
   f. you'll
   g. they'll

UNIT 17

1. a. studying
   b. planting
   c. trying
   d. digging
   e. beginning
   f. using
2. a. am
   b. was
   c. were
   d. will be
   e. was
   f. will be
3. a. digging
   b. planting
   c. raking
   d. carrying
   e. folding
   f. washing
   g. fixing
   h. wanting
   i. going
   j. using
5. a. travelled
   b. completed
   c. commenced
   d. happened
   e. arrived
   f. worked
6. a. have
   b. had
   c. will have
   d. has
   e. had
   f. will have
7. a. planted
   b. raked
   c. carried
   d. folded
   e. washed
   f. fixed
   g. wanted
   h. used
   i. mowed
   j. watered
   k. stored

UNIT 18

1. a. broken
   b. driven
   c. flown
   d. given
   e. ridden
   f. stolen
   g. taken
   h. thrown
   i. worn
   j. written
2. a. given
   b. fallen
   c. ridden
   d. taken
   e. written
3. a. have
   b. had
   c. have
   d. has
   e. have
4. a. begun
   b. dug
   c. rung
   d. sat
   e. stood
   f. swam
   g. won
   h. wound
5. a. dug
   b. sung
   c. swum
   d. won
   e. found

6. a. has
   b. had
   c. will have
   d. have
   e. had
7. a. flown
   b. taken
   c. spun
   d. begun
   e. frozen

UNIT 19

1. quickly, slowly, quickly, regularly, carefully, gradually
2. very, extremely, brightly, most, constantly
3. too, quickly, very, slowly, completely, regularly, well
5. very
   too
   carefully
   slowly
   completely/quickly
   completely/quickly/
   carefully/slowly

UNIT 20

1. slowly   how
   fast   how
   slowly   how
   last   where
   ....
   tomorrow when
   today   when
   ....
   there   where
   here   where
   ....
   why   why
   why   why
   why   why
   right   how/where
2. a. quickly
   b. first
   c. tomorrow/now
   d. there
   e. why
   f. early/now/tomorrow
   g. here
   h. carefully
   i. tomorrow/now
   j. Why
4. **Across**:
   1. quickly

3. there
4. often
7. slowly
8. yesterday
9. why
Down:
2. carefully
5. now
6. tomorrow
8. yearly

UNIT 21

1. **Prepositions**:
   a. near
   b. in
   c. on
   d. to
   e. up
   f. into
   Nouns:
   a. captain
   b. sea
   c. bike
   d. oval
   e. hill
   f. gym
2. **Prepositions**:
   a. amongst
   b. around
   c. beneath
   d. after
   e. to
   f. from
   Pronouns:
   a. us
   b. them
   c. me
   d. us
   e. her
   f. him
3. a. on, at/near, over, to/with, with
   b. in, at, in/into, between, outside
4. **Prepositions**:
   a. across, after
   b. along, in
   c. Over
   d. up
   e. down, on
   f. past
   Adverbs:
   a. past
   b. over
   c. up
   d. down

e. -
f. on, not
5. from, with, with, within, in, in, inside, at, to, near, onto into, across, down, to, after

UNIT 22

1. a. in, on, down
   b. across, under
   c. before, During, After
   d. onto, into
   e. around, beside
   f. to, from
2. In/During, onto, around, to, from
3. a. outside
   b. under
   c. off
   d. below
   e. unlike
4. a. up
   b. on
   c. Across, Along
   d. Beside, Beneath, in
   e. into, into, to

UNIT 23

1. a. her
   b. them
   c. her
   d. us
   e. you
   f. them
2. a. him, me
   b. her, him
   c. them, us
3. **Cross out**:
   a. her
   b. them
   c. them, us
   d. them
   e. us, her
   f. her, he
4. **Across**:
   2. it
   4. us
   5. him
   6. her
   7. me
   Down:
   1. you
   3. them
5. a. me/him/her/us/them
   b. me, him/her/them
   c. you, me/her/him/us/them
   d. you/him/her/them/it

WRITE WELL 3 ANSWERS

e. me/you/him/her/them, us

UNIT 24
1. a. and
   b. and, and
   c. but
   d. or
   e. yet
2. a. and
   b. and/yet
   c. He has a cat but he does not have a dog.
   d. or
   e. I didn't bring my sports shoes but I did bring my sports socks.
3. a. Both … and
   b. not … but
   c. Either … or
   d. Neither … nor
   e. as … as
4. See 3
5. a. whenever
   b. while
   c. once
   d. when
   e. since
6. See 5

UNIT 25
1. **Articles**:
   a. a, the, the, a, the
   b. the, the,
   c. a, A, the
   d. The, the, the
   e. a, the, the
2. **Nouns**:
   a. girl, swimmer, school, runner, runner
   b. athlete, hair, hurdle
   c. game, player, ball
   d. footballer, ball, goal posts
   e. turn, slippery dip, lawn
3. a. An
   b. an
   c. an
   d. an
   e. an
   f. A
   g. an
   h. a
   i. an
   j. a

UNIT 26
3. a. orange
   b. runner
   c. fighter/footballer
   d. lifesaver
   e. horse/athlete/dancer

UNIT 27
1. Mm!, Eek!, Ah!, Oops! Yuk!
2. Yuk!
   Oops!
   Mm!
   Wow!
   Eek!
   Ouch!
   Ah!/Wow!
4. Poo!
   Yuk!
   Urk!
   Phooey!

UNIT 28
1. See 2
2. a. climbed
   b. will take
   c. -
   d. is
   e. -
   f. wears
   g. has
   h. need
   i. -
   j -
   k. will come
2. **Questions**:
   a, c, d
3. **(You) subject**:
   a, c, e
4. Mark, Jill
5. a. The cat jumped over the fence.
   b. Is she wearing her new shoes?
   c. You go to the laundry.
   d. James, who is my cousin, went to Target and bought a track suit.
   e. The twins, Paul and Sandra, wear the same sort of clothes.
6. **Non-sentences**:
   She eight.
   She a new dress on.
   Yellow also.
   They … Mr Wolf?'
   Emily's … cake.
   It chocolate.
   Emily her party.
7. **Sentences**:
   She **was** eight.
   She **had** dress on.
   They **were** … also.
   They **played** … Mr Wolf?'
   Emily's grandmother **made** … cake.
   It **was** chocolate.
   Emily **loved** her party.

UNIT 29
1. a. with a long tail.
   b. in the garage
   c. during the week
   d. Because of the heavy rain
   e. over the seat
   f. to Manly
   g. with a helicopter on its decks
   h. in the morning
   i. in silence
   j. over there
   k. on Thursday afternoons
2. a. Patting Bounder the cat
   b. eating ice-cream
   c. waiting for kick-off
   d. going mountain climbing
   e. bashing into the waves
3. a. tied up all day
   b. filled with illustrations
   c. filled with water
   d. covered with snow
   e. splattered with mud
4. a. to become fitter
   b. to help their Mum
   c. to return home
   d. to earn some money
   e. to stop the glare

UNIT 30
1. He, his, him, His, he, him
2. They, their, they, their, them
3. It, It's, its
4. You, your, you, You, you
5. They, them, them, them, their
6. and, so, First, then, Afterwards

UNIT 31

UNIT 32

UNIT 33

UNIT 34
1. a. My
   b. They
   c. Can

5

d. Stop
e. There
f. When
g. It
h. Will
i. The
j. The
2. a. Australia
   b. Blue Cow
   c. Hong Kong
   d. American, Sydney Harbour
   e. Blacktown City
   f. Sleeping Beauty
   g. Simon
   h. Tiddles, Georgie Girl
   i. Portsea, Wednesday
   j. Age, Melbourne
3. a. I
   b. I'll
   c. I've, I'll
   d. I'd
   e. I
   f. I
   g. I'll
   h. I
   i. I
   j. I
4. See 5
5. Sunday, I, I, Wonderworld, He, John Smith Partners, They, I'm, Mike Jeffries, Balmain, Mum, I, What, I, You, There's, Gee, I, What, Sunday

UNIT 35

1. See 2
2. a. accountant. She …
   b. Sundays. He …
   c. Stop! You …
   d. running. We …
   e. dog. The …
   f. prize. The …
   g. friends. They …
   h. o'clock. Everything … quiet. Then …
   i. asleep. I'll …
   j. today. My …
3. a. Cres.
   b. fig.
   c. Co.
   d. Maj.
   e. Rev.
4. UK
   NZ
   WA
   SA
   RSA
   PNG
   SA
   NT
   SA
   LA
5. Mr Thomas Brown, Henry Jones & Co., 36 Gardenia Cres., Saltbush, ACT, 2607
6. NT. Dad …
   wagon. It …
   Finally …
   off. We …
   trouble. Before …
   boiled. Then …
   hot. Dad …
   it. He …
   town. I …

UNIT 36

1. a. speeding bullet? No …
   b. Can I still come?
   c. … while I'm away?
   d. Is Gary Cres. near you?
   e. …isn't it?
   f. … a good holiday.
   g. Wait a minute.
   h. … Sydney … Olympics?
   i. … I'm sixty-four?
   j. … Bali, aren't we?
2. **Questions**:
   All those sentences with a question mark (?).
4. See 5
5. Making a garden can be fun. First you have to dig the soil with a spade or a fork. When you have done that, you need to rake it. Why do you rake it? You rake it to break up the soil so you can put in your seeds and plants.

   Do you need fertiliser? Yes, fertiliser is necessary so that plants can grow well. I use cow manure because I find it the best.

   I hope you are as good a gardener as Don Burke of 'Burke's Backyard'.

UNIT 37

2. a. Stop thief!
   b. What a beautiful sweater!
   c. Ow!
   d. Look out!
   e. Oh no!
3. Eek!
   Urk!
   How beautiful!
   Wow!
   Oh no!
   Ouch!
   What a lovely day!

UNIT 38

1. a. Teeball, softball, …
   b. … a cat, a dog, …
   c. …tennis, golf, …
   d. One, two, …
   e. …2 jumpers, 4 shirts, 4 singlets,… underpants, …
   f. … lions, tigers, …
   g. dinghies, yachts, power boats, …
   h. … biscuits, canned dog food, vegetables, …
   i. … swim, … run, …cycle, …
   j. three dogs, two cats, a sick horse, a baby, kangaroo, four budgies …
2. a. …young, strong, …
   b. fat, …
   c. sad, gloomy, …
   d. young, …
   e. good, clean, …
4. a. Jessica, Thomas and Bonnie all live in the Blue Mountains.
   b. They have three dogs. They are called Bella, Roy and Arrow.
   c. Jessica loves drawing, dancing, dressing up and cooking. She also likes school.
   d. Thomas loves climbing trees, building things, using a computer and playing trains.
   e. Bonnie loves the dogs, Jessica's dolls, Tom's train and a big cardboard toy box.

UNIT 38

1. a. …Wilkins, our chemist,
   b. Ahearn, our parish priest, …
   c. White, the district nurse,
   d. yacht, 'Ragamuffin', …
   e. Elsa, the lioness, …
   f. book, *Captain Midnite*,
   g. Progress', a famous train, …
   h. Boyd, the composer, …
   i. Harris, one …singers, …

j. eucalypt, or Australian gum tree, is…
3. a. …mine,' said James.
   b. …zoo,' said Jan.
   c. …milk,' said Oliver.
   d. …Nicky,' said Oliver.
   e. …work,' said Mum.
   f. …telephone,' called Mum.
   g. …right,' whispered Julie.
   h. …pencil,' Sarah …
   i. 'The scissors, …table,' said Mum.
   j. Our teacher, Miss Young, …runner,' said Timmy.
4. 'I want to go home,' said George.
   'Don't be silly Charles,' said Betty.
   'Now pay attention,' said Mr Yates.
   'I'll now sing your favourite song,' said Lucy.
   'Woof! Woof!' said Arrow.

UNIT 40

1. a. 'I …swimming,' said …
   b. 'Do …tennis?' asked …
   c. 'Ready …go!' shouted …
   d. 'What …idea!' exclaimed …
   e. …said, 'Yes, …go.'
2. a. ' I have …cakes,' said Jim, 'and …too.'
   b. 'Have …painting?' …teacher. 'If …here.'
   c. 'Jump!' …captain, 'and …life.'
   d. 'That's …brother,' said Thomas, 'and …mum.'
   e. 'Reading is fun,' said …librarian. 'You …enjoy it.'
3. 'Am I coming …staying?'
   'You …or straying.'
   He replied, 'I …saying?'

UNIT 41

1. a. I did nothing.
      I didn't do anything.
   b. I haven't seen anyone.
      I have seen no-one.
   c. I have done nothing.
      I haven't done anything.
   d. They didn't see anyone.
      They saw no-one.
   e. We caught nothing.
      We didn't catch anything.
2. a. anyone/anybody
   b. anything
   c. anything
   d. anyone/anybody
   e. anyone/anybody
3. **Cross out:**
   a. nothing
   b. no-one
   c. nothing
4. **Plurals:**
   men
   women
   mice
   children
   teeth
   feet
   geese
   horsemen
   oxen
5. **Plurals:**
   a. calves
   b. knives
   c. leaves
   d. shelves
   e. thieves
6. **Plurals:**
   a. fairies
   b. babies
   c. daisies
   d. armies
   e. ladies

UNIT 42

1. a. Aren't, aunt
   b. aunt, aren't
   c. aren't
   d. aunt, aren't
   e. Aunt, Aren't
2. a. ate
   b. ate
   c. eight
   d. eight
   e. eight, ate
3. a. berry
   b. bury
   c. berry, berry, berry
   d. bury
   e. bury, bury
4. a. blew
   b. blue
   c. blue
   d. blew, blue
   e. blue

UNIT 43

1. a. chews
   b. Choose
   c. chews
   d. choose
   e. chews, choose
2. a. deer
   b. dear
   c. Dear
   d. dear
   e. deer
4. a. flour, flour
   b. flower
   c. flower
   d. flower
   e. flour
5. a. here
   b. hear
   c. hear
   d. here
   e. here, hear

UNIT 44

1. a. hole
   b. whole
   c. hole
   d. whole
   e. whole, hole
2. a. It's
   b. Its, its
   c. It's, its
   d. It's
   e. It's, its
4. a. knot
   b. not
   c. knot
   d. knot, not
   e. not
5. a. knows
   b. nose
   c. knows
   d. nose
   e. knows

UNIT 45

1. a. a.m.
   b. a.m.
   c. p.m.
   d. a.m.
   e. a.m., p.m.
2. a. came
   b. come
   c. came
   d. come
   e. came
3. a. good
   b. well
   c. well
   d. good
   e. well, good
4. a. learn
   b. Teach
   c. learn
   d. learn

e. teach, learn

UNIT 46

1. a. loose
   b. loose
   c. lose
   d. lose
   e. lose, loose
2. a. Can
   b. May
   c. can
   d. may, may, May
   e. May
3. a. me, my
   b. My, me
   c. my, my, my
   d. me, my
   e. My, me
4. a. of
   b. have, of
   c. have
   d. of
   e. have

UNIT 47

1. a. ran
   b. run
   c. run
   d. ran
   e. ran, run
2. a. rang
   b. rung
   c. rungs
   d. rang
   e. rung, rang
4. a. sung
   b. sang
   c. sang
   d. sung
   e. sung, sang
5. a. Those
   b. them
   c. Those
   d. them
   e. those, them

UNIT 48

1. a. began
   b. begun
   c. began
   d. began
   e. begun
2. a. came
   b. come
   c. came
   d. came

   e. come
3. a. did
   b. done
   c. done
   d. did
   e. done
4. a. ran
   b. run
   c. run
   d. run
   e. ran
5. a. rang
   b. rung
   c. rung
   d. rang
   e. rang
6. a. sang
   b. sung
   c. sung
   d. sang
   e. sang

UNIT 49

1. a. broke
   b. broken
   c. broke
   d. broken
   e. broken
2. a. drove
   b. driven
   c. drove
   d. driven
   e. driven
3. a. given
   b. gave
   c. given
   d. given
   e. given
4. a. gone
   b. went
   c. gone
   d. gone
   e. gone
5. a. ridden
   b. ridden
   c. rode
   d. ridden
   e. ridden
6. a. stolen
   b. stole
   c. stolen
   d. stolen
   e. stole

3 Circle the correlative conjunctions in these sentences.

a. Both Jim and I play football.

b. June scored not five but six goals.

c. Either Donna or Alison will make the team.

d. Neither James nor Thomas turned up for practice this afternoon.

e. I will get new running shoes as soon as I make the athletics team.

4 Write the correlative conjunctions from the sentences above.

_____

Subordinate Conjunctions

Subordinate conjunctions **join the main part of a sentence to another part of the same sentence.**

I won the race *because* I had trained for it.

5 Circle the subordinate conjunctions in these sentences.

a. I feel great whenever we win.

b. I can't play while I have a broken wrist.

c. I improved once I learned to kick properly.

d. My dog chases the cricket ball when it goes over the fence.

e. We haven't won since Bobby Jones left the team.

6 Write the subordinate conjunctions.

_____

7 Write sentences that use these conjunctions.

a. **and:** _____

b. **but:** _____

c. **as … as:** _____

d. **until:** _____

e. **once:** _____

UNIT 25 SPORT — ARTICLES A, AN, THE

There are only three articles: *a, an* and *the*.

> *a* **runner**
>
> *an* **orange**
>
> *the* **winner**

Articles describe nouns in a special way. Because they describe nouns, they are adjectives as well as articles.

THE

> *The* is called a definite article. It is definite because it points to a certain one.

> *the* **best footballer**
>
> *the* **fastest runner**
>
> *the* **winning run**

A AND AN

> *A* is called an indefinite article. It is indefinite because it does not point to a certain one:

> *A* boy could be any boy.
>
> *A* swimmer could be any swimmer.
>
> *A* dancer could be any dancer.

1 Fill in the spaces with definite or indefinite articles.

a. There is _____ girl in my class who is _____ best swimmer in _____ school. She is _____ very good runner, too. But she is not _____ fastest runner.

b. The young athlete with _____ red hair jumped _____ last hurdle.

c. Netball is _____ team game. _____ good netball player must pass _____ ball.

d. _____ footballer kicked _____ ball through _____ goal posts and everyone cheered.

e. Give me _____ turn at sliding down _____ slippery dip on _____ back lawn.

2 Draw a box around each noun which the articles describe in Exercise 1. The first one is done for you.

> *An* is an indefinite article, like *a*. You use *an* if there is a vowel following it (a,e,i,o,u).

    an **apple**   *an* **underarm throw**

It would be too hard to say *a*. (Try saying *a apple*, then say *an apple*. Which is the easier?)

3 Write *a* or *an* in the spaces.

a. _____ athlete must train hard.

b. What _____ interesting race!

c. That is _____ unimportant point.

d. Have _____ egg for breakfast.

e. I'd like to go in _____ obstacle race.

f. _____ rower has to have strong arms.

g. Would you like _____ orange?

h. I'd like to be _____ champion athlete.

i. It is _____ uphill race.

j. I was given _____ tennis racquet for Christmas.

UNIT 26 — SPORT: ARTICLES AND INTERESTING ADJECTIVES

Articles and interesting adjectives go together.

A slim, supple **and** *skilful* **gymnast**

1 Fill in the spaces with interesting adjectives from the word box. The words are in groups. Pick from any of them and add others if you wish.

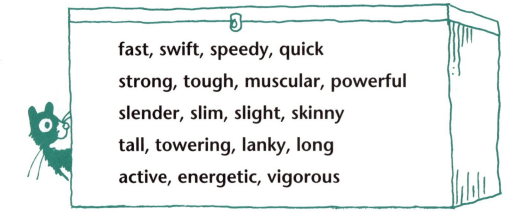

fast, swift, speedy, quick
strong, tough, muscular, powerful
slender, slim, slight, skinny
tall, towering, lanky, long
active, energetic, vigorous

a. the _____ , _____ and _____ athlete
b. a _____ , _____ and _____ weightlifter
c. an _____ , _____ and _____ sprinter
d. a _____ , _____ and _____ netball player
e. the _____ , _____ and _____ tennis player

2 Describe these things with words from the tennis ball.

Tennis ball words: crisp, painful, throbbing, lanky, juicy, ripe, lean, aching, rosy

a. _____ , _____ , _____ and _____ apple

b. the _____ , _____ , _____ ankle

c. the _____ and _____ long distance runner

3 Think of nouns to write in the spaces.

a. a ripe and juicy navel _____

b. an energetic and athletic _____

c. a rough and tough _____

d. a brown and brawny _____

e. a graceful and slender _____

4 Write articles and adjectives to describe these pictures.

_____ swimmer

_____ weightlifter

_____ dancer

_____ athletes

27 UNIT  INTERJECTIONS

Interjections show strong feelings. They have an exclamation mark after them.

(a cry of pain)   (I think that is horrible.)   (Surprise or pleasure)

We use interjections often, particularly when we are talking, but we use them in writing as well.

1 Here are some interjections. Write the ones you think should go in the speech bubbles.
EEK!   AH!   OOPS!   MMMM!   YUK!

2 Write interjections in the spaces. Choose from the clothes basket.

_____ That tastes awful.

_____ Nearly tripped.

_____ That's delicious.

_____ What a goal!

_____ Let me out of here!

_____ That hurt.

_____ That's a beautiful sweater.

Oops! Ah! Yuk! Eek! Mmm! Wow! Ouch!

3 Write five sentences which begin with these interjections.
Oh! Yuk! Mmm! Eek! Oops!

a. _____

b. _____

c. _____

d. _____

e. _____

4 Finish this story with interjections. Choose them from this list.
Urk! Poo! Phooey! Yuk!

SANDY'S SNEAKERS

Sandy had smelly sneakers. When he came into the kitchen his mother said,

'_____ Those sneakers stink. Get them in the wash.'

'_____' said his brother. 'They put me off my pizza.'

'_____' said his father. 'I think they must have died.'

'_____' said Sandy. 'They smell beautiful to me.'

59

UNIT 28 — SENTENCES AND NON-SENTENCES

Every sentence should include a finite verb. A finite verb is a verb that has a subject.

1 Circle the finite verbs. The first one is done for you. Write the finite verbs below.

a. The possum (climbed) along the power wire.
b. I will take my coat to the dry cleaners.
c. Slowly and stealthily.
d. My shirt is still on the clothes line.
e. Over the hills and far away.
f. Duncan's father wears a kilt.
g. Mum has five dresses in her cupboard.
h. I need a new jumper.
i. A ripped shirt.
j. A hole in my sock.
k. Will you come home soon?

climbed _____

_____

2 Circle those sentences that are questions.

a. Do you have a sun hat?
b. Take your sneakers off outside.
c. Going where?
d. Can I get a new pair of gym shoes?
e. You need new underpants.

3 Circle the sentences where the subject is *you* understood.

a. Get out of those filthy clothes!
b. Does Mark have another pair of shoes?
c. Find out how much it costs.
d. Is Jill coming for lunch?
e. Hurry up and get dressed.

4 Write the subject of sentences b and d in Exercise 3.

_____

5 Words have been left out of these sentences. Re-write the sentences to make them complete.

a. The cat over the fence.   _____

b. Is wearing her new dress?   _____

c. You to the laundry.   _____

d. James, who my cousin, went to Target and bought a track suit.

_____

_____

e. The twins, Paul and Sandra, the same sort of clothes.

_____

6 Read this passage and circle the non-sentences.

Emily had her birthday party on Saturday. She eight. She had five friends at her party. She a new dress on. It was yellow with a green collar. She also had new shoes. Yellow also.

Emily's dad had arranged the games. They 'Pin the Donkey', 'Balloon Volleyball', 'Treasure Hunt' and 'What's the time, Mr Wolf?'.

Emily's grandma the birthday cake. It chocolate.

All her friends took a slice home. Emily her party.

7 Write the non-sentences as sentences.

_____

_____

_____

_____

_____

UNIT 29 — RECOGNISING PHRASES

DOING THINGS

A *phrase* is a group of words with no finite verb. Some phrases begin with a preposition.

1 Circle the phrases in these sentences. Write the phrases. The first one is done for you.

a. I have a cat (with a long tail). **with a long tail**
b. We have a dinghy in the garage.
c. I play tennis during the week.
d. Because of the heavy rain, the flowers were ruined.
e. I can jump over that seat.
f. We caught the ferry to Manly.
g. We saw a navy ship with a helicopter on its deck.
h. James and Thomas are leaving in the morning.
i. We ate our meal in silence.
j. That's John's house over there.
k. I have a swimming lesson on Thursday afternoons.

Some phrases begin with a present participle or a gerund.

2 Circle the phrases in these sentences. Write the phrases. The first one is done for you.

a. (Patting Bounder the cat) is dangerous. **Patting Bounder the cat**
b. I enjoy eating ice-cream.
c. The crowd, waiting for the kick-off, became very noisy.
d. I like going mountain climbing.

e. The yacht, bashing into the waves, was moving very slowly. _____

Some phrases begin with a past participle.

3 Circle the phrases in these sentences. Write the phrases. The first one is done for you.

a. He was sad for the dog (tied up all day.)   **tied up all day**

b. Sarah took out a book filled with illustrations. _____

c. Take a glass filled with water. _____

d. We skied in an area covered with snow. _____

e. He found his car splattered with mud. _____

Some phrases begin with an infinitive.

4 Circle the phrases in these sentences. Write the phrases. The first one is done for you.

a. They exercised (to become fitter.)   **to become fitter**

b. They did it to help their mum. _____

c. She received a message to return home. _____

d. My brother works to earn some money. _____

e. He turned off the lights to stop the glare. _____

5 Write a phrase to finish each of these sentences.

a. I like _____

b. Sarah, Rachel and Mandy are all digging _____

_____

c. We caught the train _____

d. My sister has a dress _____

e. They cheered _____

UNIT 30 — DOING THINGS

COHESION: USING LINKING WORDS

1 Use other words for *John* in this passage. Choose from the box.

John likes going on exciting trips. _____ went hiking with _____ friend, Jake. Would you like to go with _____ and Jake? _____ mother often worries if _____ is safe. She is frightened something might happen to _____ .

Box: him, He, his, His, him, he

2 Use other words for *Ali, Tom* and *Lucy* in this passage. Choose from the beach ball.

Ali, Tom and Lucy went swimming. _____ went by bus to _____ friends' house so _____ could go swimming with _____ friends. Are you going swimming with _____ ?

Beach ball: They, they, their, them, their

3 Use other words for *car* in this passage. Pick from the racing car.

That car is very fast. _____ is a racing car. _____ bright red and has leather on _____ seats.

Racing car: It's, It, its

4 Use other words for *Carla* in this passage. Pick from the boat.

Words in boat: you, You, You, your, you

Come on, Carla. _____ have to come with us. Ask _____ mother if _____ can come! _____ will miss out if _____ don't ask her now.

5 Use other words for *fish* in this passage. Pick from the bowl.

The fish were swimming in the shallow water. _____ did not see us and we caught some of _____ in a net. We put _____ in a fish bowl and then we let _____ go back to _____ friends in the creek.

Words in bowl: them, them, them, their, They

6 Use linking words to finish this passage. Choose from the old ship.

Words on ship: then, so, First, and, Afterwards

Michelle _____ Tony came on holidays with us _____ I would have some friends to play with. _____ we visited the old shipwreck, _____ we ran along the beach. _____ we rode home in the bus.

7 Write two sentences using as many of these linking words as you can: so, then, after, before, and, or.

_____
_____
_____
_____

UNIT 31

DOING THINGS

NOMINAL GROUP: BUILDING WITH WORDS

A group of words which has a noun as a head word is called a *nominal group*.

In this unit you will practise building these groups, like this:

party

a party

a birthday party

a big birthday party

a big noisy birthday party

a big noisy fancy-dress birthday party

a big noisy fancy-dress birthday party on the lawn.

1 Build these nominal groups by filling in the spaces. Use the above model to help you.

a. race

_____ race

_____ cross-country race

_____ cross-country race

_____ cross-country race

_____ cross-country race

in _____ .

b. holiday

_____ holiday

_____ holiday

_____ holiday

_____ holiday

at _____ .

c. movie

_____ movie

_____ movie

_____ movie

_____ movie

about _____ .

d. forest

_____ forest

_____ forest

_____ forest

_____ forest

near _____ .

e. elephant

_____ elephant

_____ elephant

_____ elephant

_____ elephant

with _____ .

2 Fill in the spaces in these paragraphs.

a. Last _____ holidays we went on ____ _____ trip. Dad drove the _____ _____ car and we took our _____ and _____ with us. We camped on a _____ _____ beach with _____ _____ sand on it. I caught _____ _____ fish and my _____ brother caught _____ .

b. _____ _____ horses were eating hay. We went riding through the _____ forest and stopped for lunch near a _____ river. Then we rode along the _____ bank to the sea.

GENRE: RECOUNT

A *recount* tells someone what happened. When you talk about what you did at a picnic and when you write about what happened on an excursion, you are using recounts.

Here is a recount in the form of a letter.

ORIENTATION

Dear Ben,

Last week our class went to Pebbly Beach. We went to collect shells and look at the rock pools.

EVENTS

First we caught the bus to the station. Then we went by train to the National Park. Pebbly Beach is part of the park.

We saw wonderful coloured fish and anemones in the rock pools. I found a big shell that sounded like the sea.

After that, we went back to school and wrote about our excursion.

COMMENT

We had a great day.

- A recount has an opening or *orientation* which usually tells the listener or reader about the people or things involved, where it all happened and why.
- Then the *events* or happenings are described.
- A comment about the experience can be included.

The *language* (the use of words) in a recount like this one gives us *detail* and all the happenings of the day. It uses *verbs* (doing words) which are *past tense* (happened before). It has *linking words* like 'first' and 'after that' and uses *pronouns* like 'we'.

You may find other things about the language of a recount if you look at it carefully.

1 Fill in the gaps in this recount. Use your own words when you can.

THE CAMPING HOLIDAY

_____ family went _____.
_____ go there every _____.
First, we _____
_____. Then _____
_____.
We saw _____, _____ and _____.
Every morning we _____
_____. After lunch we _____
_____. It was _____ holiday.

2 Here is the opening of a recount. Write the rest of it.

Dear Penny,

We went to the zoo last week. Mr Black, our teacher, took the whole class.

First, _____
_____

Then _____
_____

After lunch _____
_____

It was _____
_____

I found out _____

3 Write down three past tense verbs from Exercise 1. Write down three linking words from Exercise 2.

_____
_____

69

UNIT 33

GENRE: INSTRUCTION

An *instruction* tells us how to do or make something. Recipes, rules for games, how to grow things are all instructions.

Here is an instruction. It tells us how to grow radishes.

Goal   **How to Grow Radishes**

                      Things you need

Materials   a well-prepared garden bed ← The language in an instruction is very clear and precise. It tells you exactly what you need and what you do.
                a rake
                a hose
                a packet of radish seed
                a hat to keep the sun off your nose

                      What to do

Steps   1   Rake garden bed carefully. ← Adverbs tell *how* a thing should be done.
           2   Make channels 1 cm deep and 15 cm apart with back of your rake.
           3   Plant seeds 3 cm apart in bottom of channels.
           4   Cover seed and press down firmly with back of rake.
           5   Water lightly with hose.
           6   Keep moist.
           7   When seedlings appear in 5–8 days, thin out if necessary.
           8   Apply liquid fertiliser every week.
           9   Pick crisp, fresh radishes after 5–7 weeks.

Commands or orders are given.

1 Write down three things that are needed to grow radishes.

a. _____

b. _____

c. _____

2 Write down one order that is given.

_____

3 Write down three adverbs that tell you how a thing should be done.

_____

4 Here is a list of things you will need to boil an egg and a list of commands about what you should do. Write an instruction called *How to Boil an Egg*.
Use the model *How to Grow Radishes* to help you.

Materials: ½ litre of water, 1 small saucepan, 1 egg.
Steps: Fill the saucepan with ½ litre of water; bring to boil; put egg in water with spoon; boil for 4 minutes; turn off the stove; drain saucepan; serve egg in eggcup.

Goal _____

Materials _____

_____

_____

Steps

1. _____
2. _____
3. _____
4. _____
5. _____
6. _____
7. _____

5 Finish some of these types of instructions. You will be able to think of many kinds.

a. How to Cook _____
b. How to Play _____
c. How to Grow _____
d. How to Ride _____
e. How to Eat _____

6 More to Do In your own book, write the instructions for one of the above.

UNIT 34 — DOING THINGS: USING CAPITAL LETTERS

Capital letters begin sentences.

1 Correct these sentences by using capital letters where required. Write the words you have changed in the spaces. The first one is done for you.

a. My dog was hit by a car.　　　　　　　　　**My**

b. We like going on picnics. they are always fun.　　　_____

c. can we go to the zoo on Sunday?　　　_____

d. stop that at once!　　　_____

e. there is something eating my lettuce.　　　_____

f. Is that book from the library? when did you get it?　　　_____

g. No I won't. it just isn't right.　　　_____

h. will you be home on Wednesday?　　　_____

i. the car, which is quite old, needs new tyres.　　　_____

j. the sun rises at 5.45 a.m. and sets at 5.30 p.m.　　　_____

Capital letters are used for proper nouns.

2 Put capital letters on the proper nouns in these sentences.

a. australia has mild winters.

b. We went skiing at blue cow.

c. My friend lives in hong kong.

d. An american warship sailed into sydney harbour.

e. My friends and I play football for blacktown city.

f. We went to see the movie sleeping beauty.

g. My brother's name is simon.

h. Our cat is called tiddles and our dog is georgie girl.

i. Are you going to portsea on wednesday?

j. The age is a melbourne morning newspaper.

> **The personal pronoun *I* is always written with a capital letter.**

3 Correct these sentences by using capital letters where required. Write down the words you have changed.

a. James and i go to school together. _____

b. I think i'll go home now. _____

c. When i've finished my homework, i'll watch TV. _____

d. I know i'd like to go to Fiji. _____

e. Maybe i should have stayed at home. _____

f. 'Can i go to the movies?' _____

g. Some day i'll be able to buy that bike. _____

h. Robin, Emily, Henry, Peter and i are very good friends. _____

i. How can i get away from here? _____

j. i quit! _____

4 Correct this passage by putting in all the capital letters.

NOTHING TO DO

It was sunday and there was nothing to do. i was bored stiff. My brother and i were going to wonderworld but at the last minute my father had to go to work. he works for john smith and partners. they are architects. He was disappointed he had to go but he always says that.

'i'm picking up mike jeffreys at his home in balmain,' he told mum.

'i don't expect to be home till tea time.'

'what can i do?' I asked mum.

'you can help me,' she said. 'there's plenty to do.'

'gee thanks,' i said. 'what a fun sunday!'

5 Write down the words you have changed.

_____

_____

UNIT 35 — DOING THINGS: USING FULL STOPS

A full stop ends a sentence which is a statement or a command. Some short commands may have an exclamation mark.

1 Add full stops and capital letters to these sentences. Use the symbol [⊙] to show where the full stops go. The first one is done for you.

a. My mum's an accountant ⊙ She works in the city.

b. Dad plays squash on Sundays he plays tennis on Wednesdays.

c. Stop you can't go in there.

d. The family likes running we are all entered in the City to Surf race.

e. The cat scratched the dog the dog ran away.

f. If I win, I get a trip as the prize the prize is worth $2000.

g. Josh and Mandy are friends they both like playing golf.

h. Seven o'clock everything is quiet then, suddenly there's a loud roar.

i. Is Rachel home? Yes, but she's still asleep i'll wake her up.

j. I'm ten today my brother is only seven.

2 Write the word *before* and the word *after* the full stop. The first one is done for you.

accountant. She

_____   _____   _____

_____   _____   _____

_____   _____

Full stops are used to show abbreviated words where the last letter is not part of the abbreviation *Captain—Capt.*

3 Write the abbreviated form of the highlighted words.

a. I live in Jamieson **Crescent**. _____

b. Refer to **figure** 3 on page 62. _____

c. Tom works for Boling and **Company**. _____

74

PGH 57

d. **Major** Senek is in the army. _____

e. **Reverend** Henderson is still our minister. _____

> If a name which is made up of more than one word is shortened, the first letter of each word is used. There are no full stops between the letters.   United States of America—USA

4 Write the abbreviated form of the following places.

United Kingdom	____	Papua New Guinea	____
New Zealand	____	South Australia	____
Western Australia	____	Northern Territory	____
South America	____	Saudi Arabia	____
Republic of South Africa	____	Los Angeles	____

5 Put in full stops where they are needed.

Mr Thomas Brown,
Henry Jones & Co ,
36 Gardenia Cres ,
Saltbush, ACT, 2607

6 Correct this passage, putting in all the full stops and capital letters where required.

OUR TRIP

We went for a trip to Alice Springs in the NT dad had spent a lot of time working on our four-wheel drive station wagon it would need to be in good repair for this trip.

finally, the day arrived and we set off we soon ran into some trouble before we were out of town, the engine had boiled then the brakes got too hot dad couldn't believe it he really got angry. Anyway, with a bit of help, we made it out of town. i was very happy for dad.

75

36 UNIT — DOING THINGS: USING QUESTION MARKS

The question mark is used at the end of a sentence which is a question.

1 Add question marks, full stops and capital letters to these sentences. The first one is done for you.

a. Is it a speeding bullet? No, it's superman.

b. Can i still come

c. Will you look after my garden while i'm away

d. Is Gary Cres near you

e. Forest Road is the main road, isn't it

f. I hope you have a good holiday

g. Wait a minute

h. Did you think sydney would get the 2000 olympics

i. Will you still need me when i'm sixty-four

j. We're flying QANTAS to bali, aren't we

2 Write the questions below.

_____
_____
_____
_____
_____
_____
_____
_____

3 Write down five questions about going to the Museum.

a. _____
b. _____

c. _____
d. _____
e. _____

4 Edit this passage putting all the punctuation in to make it correct.

MAKING A GARDEN

Making a garden can be fun first you have to dig the soil with a spade or a fork when you've done that you need to rake it. Why do you rake it you rake it to break up the soil so you can put in your seeds and plants.

Do you need fertiliser yes, fertiliser is necessary so that plants can grow well i use cow manure because i find it the best.

I hope you are as good a gardener as don burke of 'burke's backyard'.

5 Write out the edited copy of 'Making a Garden'.

UNIT 37 — USING EXCLAMATION MARKS

If you exclaim, you call out. Exclamation marks are needed to show this in writing. You call out if you are excited or angry—in fact, any time you show strong feelings.

All interjections are exclamations and need an exclamation mark, as you found in Unit 27.

So, *Wow! Oh!* and *Ouch!* need exclamation marks.

Exclamation marks are needed with short commands.

So, *Halt! Jump!* and *Get out!* need exclamation marks.

Remember, all expressions of strong feelings need exclamation marks.

1 Put in exclamation marks where they are needed. There are boxes to help you.

a. Wow ☐   What a beautiful track suit ☐

b. Ouch ☐   That hurt ☐

c. Stop ☐

d. What a great win ☐

e. How terrible ☐

2 Write the exclamation which would suit each situation. Pick from the box.

a. A policeman yells to a thief. _____

b. You are admiring someone's sweater. _____

c. You have just hurt your toe. _____

d. What you would say if someone was in your way. _____

e. What you would say if you made a mistake. _____

Box: Look out! Ow! What a beautiful sweater! Oh no! Stop thief!

3 Here are the descriptions of some strong feelings you might have. Write an exclamation beside each one. Pick the right exclamations from the box.

You are frightened. _____

You are disgusted. _____

You think something is very pretty. _____

You are surprised and pleased. _____

You get a disappointment and a shock. _____

Something hurts you. _____

You wake up and the sun is shining. _____

How beautiful!
Wow!
Oh no!
Eek!
Urk!
What a lovely day!
Ouch!

UNIT 38 — DOING THINGS: USING COMMAS

A comma is used in a sentence to give a short pause and to help make the meaning clearer.

1 Put commas where they are needed in the following sentences. The first one is done for you.

a. Teeball**,** softball and baseball are similar games.

b. We have a cat a dog a canary and a goldfish.

c. I play tennis golf cricket and hockey.

d. One two three and they're off.

e. I have 2 jumpers 4 shirts 4 singlets 4 pairs of underpants 3 pairs of socks but only one pair of shoes.

f. We saw lions tigers giraffes and monkeys at the zoo.

g. At the Boat Show, we looked at dinghies yachts power boats rubber duckies and sailboards.

h. My dog likes biscuits canned dog food vegetables eggs and bananas.

i. On Monday I swim on Tuesday I run on Wednesday I cycle on Thursday I dance and on Friday I go to the gym.

j. My dad's a vet. Last Saturday he treated three dogs two cats a sick horse a baby kangaroo four budgies and a tortoise. I think he's pretty clever.

2 Put in commas where they are needed.

a. My horse is a young strong chestnut filly.

b. He's too fat too unfit and too unhealthy to run in the race.

c. It's a sad gloomy depressing painting.

d. She's young good looking and very happy.

e. It was a good clean fair race.

3 Finish these sentences.

a. The acts I most enjoyed at the circus were _____

_____

b. For dinner we had _____
   _____ and _____
c. We went to _____
   and _____ when we were travelling around our state.
d. In my school bag I have _____
   _____

e. The four shows I most enjoy on
   television are _____
   _____
   and _____
   _____

4 Use full stops, commas and capital letters to edit these sentences. Write the edited sentences underneath.

a. Jessica thomas and Bonnie all live in the blue mountains
   _____

b. They have three dogs they are called bella roy and arrow
   _____

c. Jessica loves drawing dancing dressing up and cooking she also likes school
   _____
   _____

d. Thomas loves climbing trees building things using a computer and playing trains
   _____
   _____

e. Bonnie loves the dogs Jessica's dolls tom's train and a big cardboard toy box
   _____
   _____

PGH 59

MORE USING COMMAS

Commas are used to separate ideas in a sentence.

1 Put commas in these sentences. The first one is done for you.

a. Mr Wilkins**,** our chemist**,** has his shop in the city.
b. Father Ahearn our parish priest comes from Ireland.
c. Sister White the district nurse is my auntie.
d. A famous yacht 'Ragamuffin' is moored in the bay.
e. Elsa the lioness was the star of the film *Born Free*.
f. The book *Captain Midnite* is about a bushranger.
g. 'The Spirit of Progress' a famous train used to run between Sydney and Melbourne.
h. Anne Boyd the composer is also a fine flute player.
i. Rolf Harris one of Australia's best-loved singers is visiting our school next week.
j. The eucalypt or Australian gum tree is widely grown in California.

2 Complete these sentences. Use commas to punctuate them correctly.

a. _____ our butcher _____

b. _____ an Australian marsupial _____

c. _____ our family doctor _____

d. The bank we use _____ gives the best service.

e. _____ my black and white dog is the greatest.

Commas are used to mark off direct speech.

3 Put in the commas in this direct speech. The first one is done for you.

a. 'That cat is mine,' said James.
b. 'Today we're going to the zoo' said Jan.
c. 'I like milk' said Oliver.
d. 'Give this present to Nicky' said Oliver.
e. 'Rachel is at work' said mum.
f. 'Someone answer the telephone' called mum.
g. 'I'm all right' whispered Julie.
h. 'I haven't a pen or a pencil' Sarah told her teacher.
i. 'The scissors sticky tape and brown paper are already on the table' said mum.
j. 'Our teacher Miss Young is a marathon runner' said Timmy.

4 Write what each person is saying as direct speech. The first one is done for you.

George — I want to go home.

'I want to go home,' said George.

Betty — Don't be silly, Charles.

_____

Mr Yates — Now pay attention.

Lucy — I'll now sing your favourite song.

_____

Arrow — Woof! Woof!

_____

UNIT 40 — DOING THINGS: QUOTATION MARKS

' ... '

Quotation marks tell us what is said.

'I like hiking,' said Louise.

*You may use double quotation marks ("...") if you like.

1 Write the quotation marks in these sentences.

a. I like swimming, said Dino.

b. Do you like tennis? asked Mary.

c. Ready, set, go! shouted the starter.

d. What a good idea! exclaimed the teacher.

e. My dad said, Yes, you can go.

Sometimes, what is being said is in different parts of a sentence like this:

'I like swimming,' said Dino, 'and I like riding my bike'.

2 Write the quotation marks in these sentences.

a. I can make cakes, said Jim, and I can cook eggs, too.

b. Have you finished your painting? asked the teacher. If you have, bring it out here.

c. Jump! yelled the captain, and run for your life.

d. That's my brother, said Thomas, and that's my mum.

e. Reading is fun, said the librarian. You will enjoy it.

3 Write the quotation marks in this poem.

A REMARKABLY WOOLLY DOG

I met on the corner while playing
A remarkably woolly dog, straying.
His tail, sides and head
Looked the same and he said,
Am I coming, or going or staying?

So I said to this woolly dog, straying,
You are coming, not going or staying.
He replied, I can't hear
If you talk to my rear.
What was it again you were saying?

Gordon Winch

A POINT TO NOTICE

You do not need quotation marks with indirect speech, like this:
The woolly dog said that he did not know if he was coming or going or staying.

UNIT 41  DOUBLE NEGATIVES, NOUN PLURALS

DOUBLE NEGATIVES

| **ALWAYS say** | *I didn't do anything.* | **(CORRECT)** |
| **NEVER say** | *I didn't do nothing.* | **(INCORRECT)** |

The second one is a double negative.

1 Here are some examples of sentences containing double negatives. Write the sentences correctly in the spaces.

a. I never did nothing.

_____

b. I haven't seen no-one.

_____

c. I haven't done nothing.

_____

d. They didn't see no-one.

_____

e. We didn't catch nothing.

_____

2 Fill in the spaces with words from the box.

a. I didn't see _____ when I went walking.

b. They haven't won _____ .

c. We didn't do _____ .

d. She hasn't met _____ .

e. He didn't talk to _____ .

3 Cross out the wrong words.

a. We didn't eat (nothing, anything).

b. I haven't seen (no-one, anyone).

c. She didn't take (anything, nothing).

anything anyone anything anybody anyone

86

NOUN PLURALS

Some nouns change their spelling in the plural.

4 Write the plurals of these words in the spaces. The first one is done for you.

SINGULAR	PLURAL	SINGULAR	PLURAL
man	**men**	foot	_____
woman	_____	goose	_____
mouse	_____	horseman	_____
child	_____	ox	_____
tooth	_____		

Others change *f* or *fe* to *v* and add *es*.

5 Write the plurals of these words in the spaces. The first one is done for you.

a. The (calf) __**calves**__ were hungry.
b. The (knife) _____ were sharp
c. The (leaf) _____ were green.
d. The (shelf) _____ were empty.
e. The (thief) _____ were caught.

Others that end in *y*, with another consonant in front, change the *y* to *i* and add *es*.

6 Write the plurals of these words in the spaces. The first one is done for you.

a. The (fairy) __**fairies**__ were dancing on the lawn.
b. The (baby) _____ were crying.
c. The (daisy) _____ were growing.
d. The (army) _____ were marching.
e. The (lady) _____ were visiting.

UNIT 42 — DOING THINGS: HOMONYMS: AREN'T, AUNT; AND OTHERS

Homonyms cause trouble in writing. We need to practise using them correctly.

aren't aunt

Aren't is a contraction of *are not*.
An *aunt* is the sister of your mother or father.

1 Fill in the correct **aren't aunt** homonyms.

a. _____ you going to visit your _____ ?

b. My _____ and uncle _____ living here now.

c. They _____ very interested in making things.

d. My _____ is older than my mother but she has the same coloured hair. You will find it hard to tell them apart if you _____ careful.

e. _____ Tracy is coming to the football match. _____ you?

ate eight

Ate is part of the verb *to eat*.
Eight is the number after seven.

2 Fill in the correct **ate eight** homonyms.

a. Who _____ the sandwich?

b. If you _____ it, own up.

c. There were _____ boys and seven girls at the party.

d. The number _____ comes before nine.

e. The _____ children _____ all of the pies.

Where is the cake?

I ate it.

berry bury

A *berry* is a small fruit.
To *bury* means to cover with earth.

3 Fill in the correct **berry bury** homonyms.

a. The bird ate the _____ .

b. I saw the squirrel _____ the nuts.

c. This _____ is blue; this _____ is black and this _____ is red. They are all good to eat.

d. Dogs often _____ bones.

e. If you _____ the seed in the ground it will sprout in the spring. Don't _____ it too far down, though.

blew blue

Blew **is part of the verb** *to blow.*
Blue **is the colour, blue. It can mean** *unhappy,* **too.**

4 Fill in the correct **blew blue** homonyms.

a. The wind _____ in my face.

b. I have a beautiful _____ sweater.

c. I feel _____ today.

d. I _____ out all the candles on my birthday cake. It had eight candles and bright _____ icing.

e. When you feel _____ , you are unhappy.

5 Write a sentence for each of these words: **aren't, aunt, ate, eight, berry, bury, blew, blue.**

a. _____

b. _____

c. _____

d. _____

e. _____

f. _____

g. _____

h. _____

UNIT 43 — DOING THINGS
HOMONYMS: CHEWS, CHOOSE; AND OTHERS

chews choose

Chews is part of the verb *to chew,* meaning to grind food up with your teeth.

Choose is part of the verb *to choose,* meaning to decide which one you will have.

1 Fill in the correct **chews choose** homonyms.

a. My puppy _____ bones.

b. _____ between the pink and the blue.

c. He _____ his food slowly.

d. If you _____ that road you will get lost.

e. He _____ the red apple. You _____ one that you would like to chew.

dear deer

Dear means someone you love. It can also mean costing a great deal. *Deer* is an animal.

2 Fill in the correct **dear deer** homonyms.

a. Some _____ have antlers on their heads.

b. She is my _____ friend.

c. The letter began, _____ Mr Smith.

d. This meat is very _____ ; I'll have something cheaper.

e. There was a herd of _____ in the forest.

3 Write a sentence for each of these words: **chews, choose, dear, deer.**

a. _____

b. _____

c. _____

d. _____

flour flower

Flour is used for making bread and cakes. It is made from wheat and other grain.

A *flower* is the blossom of a plant.

4 Fill in the correct **flour flower** homonyms.

a. White bread is made from white _____ ;

   brown bread is made from brown _____ .

b. A rose is a beautiful _____ .

c. Bees come to this _____ to collect pollen.

d. Dad was working in the _____ bed.

e. In this recipe you need two cups of _____ .

hear here

Hear is what your ear does.

Here is an adverb which points out a place.

5 Fill in the correct **hear here** homonyms.

a. Come _____ at once!

b. Can you _____ the music?

c. They could _____ the children singing.

d. It is not there, it is _____ .

e. If you come over _____ you will be able to _____ the

   sounds of the ocean.

6 Write a sentence for each of these words: **flour, flower, hear, here.**

a. _____

b. _____

c. _____

d. _____

UNIT 44 — DOING THINGS
HOMONYMS: HOLE, WHOLE; AND OTHERS

hole whole

Hole is an opening in something.
Whole means all of a thing.

1 Fill in the correct **hole whole** homonyms.

a. There is a _____ in my sock and my toe peeps through.

b. I ate the _____ orange.

c. There is a _____ in the bucket.

d. The _____ class went to the museum.

e. You will need a _____ barrow load of

earth to fill the _____ in the ground.

its it's

Its is a pronoun and an adjective (pronominal adjective). *Its* shows ownership. It does not have an apostrophe.

Its coat was long.

It's is a contraction of 'it is'. An apostrophe is needed to show that a letter is left out.

It's a hot day.

2 Fill in the correct **its it's** homonyms.

a. _____ fun to play in the park.

b. _____ coat is brown and _____ tail is long.

c. _____ time for _____ food.

d. _____ going to be interesting at the aquarium.

e. Is that your dog? _____ chewing my shoe. Pull _____ lead, will you!

3 Write a sentence for each of these words: **hole, whole, its, it's.**

a. _____

b. _____

c. _____

d. _____

knot not

A *knot* is something you tie in a piece of rope, string or other material.
Not is the no adverb.
I will *not* go.

4 Fill in the correct **knot not** homonyms.

a. Tie a _____ in the rope.

b. I will _____ jump over that fence.

c. You will need a double _____ in your shoelace.

d. It is hard to tie a _____ in a fishing line;

you must make certain that it does _____ slip.

e. No, that is _____ my favourite sport.

knows nose

Knows is part of the verb *to know*.
Your *nose* is in the middle of your face.

5 Fill in the correct **knows nose** homonyms.

a. He _____ that he will be in the team.

b. His _____ is sunburnt.

c. Jillian _____ all of her spelling.

d. The anteater has a long _____ .

e. It _____ that you are in the forest because it can smell your

scent with its sensitive _____ .

6 Write a sentence for each of these words: **knot, not, knows, nose.**

a. _____

b. _____

c. _____

d. _____

UNIT 45 — CONFUSED WORDS: A.M. P.M.; AND OTHERS

DOING THINGS

Some pairs of words, which are not homonyms, are often confused. It is hard to tell the difference between them. We need to practise using them correctly.

a.m. p.m.

a.m. is the time from midnight to the middle of the day.
p.m. is the time from the middle of the day to midnight.

1 Write **a.m.** or **p.m.** in the spaces. Fill in the time where it is needed, also.

   8.00 a.m. is when we have breakfast.

a. I go to bed at 8.30 _____

b. after breakfast   _____ _____

c. after tea   _____ _____

d. Time to get up : it's 7.00 _____ .

e. My father gets up at 6.30 _____ and goes to bed at 10.30 _____ .

came come

Came is the past tense of the verb to come (what happened in the past).
Come is the past participle of that verb (the part that goes with *has, have* or *had*).

2 Write the correct words in the spaces.

a. I _____ to see them.

b. They have _____ to see us.

c. She _____ to watch us play.

d. My mother has _____ to watch, too.

e. He _____ from overseas.

good well

Good is an adjective in most cases. It describes a noun.
Well is an adverb. It adds meaning to a verb.

3 Write the correct words in the spaces.

a. You are a _____ boy.

b. How are you? I am feeling _____ .

c. How did they play? They played _____ .

d. It was a very _____ game.

e. She played _____ and took some _____ catches.

learn teach

When you *learn,* you take something in.
When you *teach,* you give something out.

4 Write the correct words in the spaces.

a. Did you _____ your spelling?

b. _____ me how to swim.

c. If you _____ how to swim, you will be safe.

d. I am going to _____ how to speak a foreign language.

e. I will _____ you. See if you can _____ quickly.

5 Write a sentence for each of these:
a.m., p.m., came, come, good, well, learn, teach.

a. _____
b. _____
c. _____
d. _____
e. _____
f. _____
g. _____
h. _____

UNIT 46 — DOING THINGS: CONFUSED WORDS: LOSE, LOOSE; AND OTHERS

lose loose

Lose is a verb meaning *to mislay something* (*mislay* means you cannot find it).
Loose is usually an adjective describing something as in *a loose shirt*.

1 Write the correct words in the spaces.

a. My socks are _____ ; they keep falling down.

b. The nut is _____ . Tighten it before the wheel falls off.

c. Where did you _____ your bag?

d. I tried to _____ him in the crowd.

e. You will easily _____ your hat if it is too _____ .

can may

Can means you are able to do something.

        I *can* jump that fence.

It means *a can* as in a can of Coke, too.

May means that there is a chance that you will.

        I *may* see you at the gym.

It can also mean you are allowed to do something.

        Mum said that I *may* play.

May is also the month of May.

2 Write the correct words in the spaces.

a. _____ you draw a boat?

b. _____ I be excused?

c. They _____ really play tennis.

d. I _____ come or I _____ not; it depends on the weather and the month. _____ will be the best.

e. _____ I eat these chips?

me my

Me is a personal pronoun.
My is a pronoun and a pronominal adjective. It shows possession (ownership).
You do NOT say *me book*.

3 Write the correct words in the spaces.

a. He hit _____ because he thought _____ ball was his.

b. _____ brother is like _____ .

c. He is _____ uncle, she is _____ cousin and that is _____ dog.

d. Give _____ the book and I will put it in _____ bag.

e. _____ favourite sport is swimming; it just suits _____ .

have of

Have is a verb.
Of is a preposition.
You NEVER say *could of* or *should of*.

4 Write the correct words in the spaces.

a. What a big box _____ apples!

b. I could _____ eaten two _____ them.

c. We lost the match; we should _____ won.

d. Six cans _____ drink, please.

e. I will _____ won six matches if I win tomorrow.

5 Write a sentence for each of these words: **loose, lose, can, may, me, my, could have.**

a. _____

b. _____

c. _____

d. _____

e. _____

f. _____

g. _____

UNIT 47 — CONFUSED WORDS: RAN, RUN; AND OTHERS

DOING THINGS

ran run

These two words are both parts of the verb *to run*.
Ran is the past tense (time) and is found by itself; *run* is the past participle. It must have the word *has, have* or *had* with it.
Run can also be a noun: He scored a *run*.

1 Write the correct words in the spaces.

a. I _____ up the street.

b. He has _____ a very fast race.

c. Have you _____ in the City to Surf race?

d. The mouse _____ up the clock.

e. He _____ up the pitch and scored a quick _____ .

rang rung

Rang is the past tense of the verb to ring. *Rung* is the past participle; it must have the word *has, have* or *had* with it.
Rung can also be a noun: a *rung* in the ladder.

2 Write the correct words in the spaces.

a. He _____ me yesterday.

b. Has he _____ you?

c. That ladder has five _____ .

d. I _____ him to see if he was coming to school.

e. They have _____ the bell seven times; I _____ it eight times yesterday.

3 Write a sentence for each of these words: **ran, run, rang, rung.**

a. _____

b. _____

c. _____

d. _____

sang sung

Sang is the past tense of the verb to sing. Sung is the past participle. It must have the word *has*, *have* or *had* with it.

4 Write the correct words in the spaces

a. I have _____ with the choir.

b. He _____ with it, too.

c. They _____ beautifully.

d. Has she _____ to you?

e. They had _____ many times, but
   I _____ only once.

them those

Them is a personal pronoun.

    I saw *them*.

Those can be a pronoun or a pronominal adjective.

    Those are my books.   (PRONOUN)
    Those books are mine.   (ADJECTIVE)

5 Write the correct words in the spaces.

a. _____ football boots are muddy.

b. I took _____ to see the teacher.

c. _____ are mine.

d. Don't take it from _____ .

e. I gave _____ apples to _____ .

6 Write a sentence for each of these words: **sang, sung, them, those.**

a. _____

b. _____

c. _____

d. _____

99

UNIT 48 — CONFUSED WORDS: BEGAN, BEGUN AND OTHERS

Doing Things

Began and *begun* are past forms of 'to begin', e.g. I *began*, I have *begun*.

1. Circle the correct words in these sentences.

a. I (began, begun) school when I was five.

b. We have (began, begun) swimming lessons.

c. James (began, begun) painting the fence last Saturday.

d. Christine (began, begun) to shiver. It was very cold.

e. Bindi had (began, begun) a new job.

Came and *come* are past forms of 'to come', e.g. I *came*, I have *come*.

2. Circle the correct words in these sentences.

a. When I (came, come) home, I took off my shoes.

b. Jeffrey has (came, come) to have a meal with us.

c. The cat (came, come) home with a dead rat.

d. If Harry (came, come), he could sleep on the sofa.

e. William and Sally have (came, come) to see the new baby.

Did and *done* are past forms of 'to do', e.g. I *did*, I have *done*.

3. Circle the correct words in these sentences.

a. I (did, done) my homework last night.

b. Have you (did, done) the washing up yet?

c. Edward has (did, done) all the hard work.

d. Darcy (did, done) the vacuum cleaning.

e. Chester has (did, done) everything his dad asked him to do.

Ran **and** *run* **are past forms of 'to run', e.g. I** *ran,* **I have** *run.*

4 Use **ran** or **run** to complete these sentences.

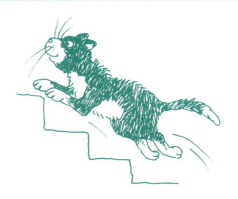

a. The cat _____ up the stairs.

b. I have _____ five kilometres.

c. The class has _____ around the playground twice.

d. Charles has _____ away from home.

e. They _____ until they couldn't stand up.

Rang **and** *rung* **are past forms of 'to ring', e.g. I** *rang,* **I have** *rung.*

5 Use **rang** or **rung** to complete these sentences.

a. The bell _____ at half past nine.

b. Has your teacher ever _____ home?

c. They have _____ seven times this week.

d. The church bells _____ out across the countryside.

e. I _____ the bell yesterday.

Sang **and** *sung* **are past forms of 'to sing', e.g. I** *sang,* **I have** *sung.*

6 Use **sang** or **sung** to complete these sentences.

a. The birds _____ in the trees this morning.

b. Jill has _____ that song many times.

c. They have _____ all the songs they know.

d. George _____ the National Anthem at the District Sports Day.

e. Pauline, Phillip and Pat _____ in the school choir last Saturday.

UNIT 49 — DOING THINGS: CONFUSED WORDS: BROKE, BROKEN AND OTHERS

Broke and *broken* are past forms of 'to break', e.g. I *broke*, I have *broken*.

1 Circle the correct words in these sentences.

a. I (broke, broken) that window.

b. John has (broke, broken) his arm in two places.

c. William and Gertie have (broke, broken) that valuable vase.

d. You have (broke, broken) your promise to me.

e. Have the prisoners (broke, broken) out of prison?

Drove and *driven* are past forms of 'to drive', e.g. I *drove*, I have *driven*.

2 Circle the correct words in these sentences.

a. Mum (drove, driven) home last night.

b. Mum has (drove, driven) grandma over to see her sister.

c. 'They have (drove, driven) me mad today,' said the teacher.

d. Will they have (drove, driven) all the way from Brisbane?

e. Have you (drove, driven) a Ford lately?

Gave and *given* are past forms of 'to give', e.g. I *gave*, I have *given*.

3 Circle the correct words in these sentences.

a. I have (gave, given) him until tomorrow to return my pen.

b. Jane, Betty and Sarah each (gave, given) a $1 donation.

c. Brian and Terry have (gave, given) their pocket money as a donation.

d. She has (gave, given) her best effort.

e. You have always (gave, given) very generously.

Went and *gone* are past forms of 'to go', e.g. I *went*, I *have gone*.

4 Use **went** or **gone** to complete these sentences.

a. The creek has _____ down since last night.

b. Uncle Jack _____ into town to buy a new tractor.

c. Billy and Fred have _____ to the football.

d. Has Jane _____ to the movies?

e. The bell has _____ .

Rode and *ridden* are past forms of 'to ride', e.g. I *rode*, I *have ridden*.

5 Use **rode** or **ridden** to complete these sentences.

a. The young jockey has _____ two winners.

b. Have you _____ in the new car yet?

c. I _____ in the last carriage of the train.

d. Ben and Sandy have _____ on the merry-go-round three times without paying.

e. She has _____ that horse in the local show.

Stole and *stolen* are past forms of 'to steal', e.g. I *stole*, I *have stolen*.

6 Use **stole** or **stolen** to complete these sentences.

a. Has there been anything _____ ?

b. The thief _____ nearly a hundred dollars from my grandad.

c. You have _____ my ruler, haven't you?

d. Barbara and Brian have _____ away from the party.

e. It is I who _____ your pencil. I thought it was mine.

CHECKLIST

Here is a checklist so you can mark off what you have successfully completed in this book.

You will notice that there are two columns. The first column is a list of all the material covered in the *Write Well* series 4–6. You will notice that some of the squares are shaded. Those that are indicate the material covered at this level. These are the only squares you will be interested in.

The second column is left blank. When you have successfully completed a unit you should go to this checklist and tick the content you have just completed.

ADJECTIVES		
• descriptive		
• numeral/number		
• pronominal		
possessive	▓	
demonstrative		
distributive		
interrogative		
indefinite		
emphatic		
reflexive		
• degree	▓	
positive	▓	
comparative	▓	
superlative	▓	
ADVERBS		
• degree in adverbs		
• kinds:		
interrogative		
manner	▓	
negative		
place		
reason		
time		
ARTICLES		
• definite		
• indefinite		
ATTRIBUTES		
CIRCUMSTANCES		
CLAUSES		
• principal		
• subordinate		
adjectival		
adverbial		
noun		

COHESION		
• conjunctions		
• ellipsis		
• reference	▓	
• synonyms		
CONFUSED WORDS	▓	
CONJUNCTIONS	▓	
• co-ordinate		
• correlative		
• subordinate	▓	
DOUBLE NEGATIVES		
GENRE		
• argument		
• explanation		
• instruction	▓	
• narrative		
• recount	▓	
• report		
GERUNDS		
HOMONYMS	▓	
INTERJECTIONS	▓	
NOMINAL GROUP		
NOMINALISATION		
NOUNS		
• case		
• gender	▓	
• number	▓	
• person		
NOUNS	▓	
• abstract	▓	
• collective		
• common		
• proper	▓	
PARTICIPANTS		